Pr

"Intuitive and easy-to-read overview of the nuts and bolts of running a business. A must-read for entrepreneurs on how to give structure to a business."

Kevin Sullivan
CEO, Daxbot

"From the very first chapters, I knew the principles outlined in this book were transformative. I couldn't wait to integrate them into my company."

John Cassidy
Founder, Mountain Grounds Artisan Roastery

"If given one book to structure my business for growth, I'd want it to be *The Framework*. It's immediately applicable and provides confidence and clarity."

Tony Sollars
CEO, WatchTower IT Solutions

"*The Framework* provides an actionable approach to building a more structured business. With practical tools, it delivers useful insights for leaders seeking to create a strong culture and improve team performance."

Tyler Redden
Founder, Red N Solutions

THE FRAMEWORK

HOW A FEW SIMPLE PRINCIPLES TRANSFORMED A BUSINESS FOREVER

JASON RICHARDS

© 2024 Jason Richards

Published by Leadcademy Publishing.

ISBN: 9798337723808 (Hardcover)

ISBN: 9798335303682 (Paperback)

Printed in the United States of America

This book is dedicated to my friend and mentor:

Alan Branham

He lived a life worth exemplifying,
pushed me in my faith and
showed me what was possible.

Contents

Preface

READ ME FIRST! – How to get the most from this book

Read the first three chapters. If it resonates, move forward. If it doesn't resonate, then this book isn't for you!

Here are some suggestions on how to get the most out of this book, depending on your personality:

1) **I want help with this** – Go to Part Two and see how The Framework could benefit your company. If you want help implementing The Framework, we would be glad to see if a Framework Coach would fit your situation well. Please send an email to info@leadcademy.com.

2) **Just give me the checklists** – Start with Part Three, download the ToolKit, and go through the meetings with your team as outlined below. Get everyone on the team a copy of the book and have everyone read the chapters before you meet so that you can make the most of your discussion.

3) **I love to read and figure it out myself** - Read the book from start to finish. Read the story completely first to understand the journey you will take. Get everyone on the team a copy of the book, and then download the ToolKit to go through the book with your team as outlined below.

Regardless of personality type, implementing The Framework is best done over 90 days with three full-day, off-site meetings with your team. We use this process with clients, and it's the same process you see Alan go through with the Reynolds Industries team.

Meeting off-site (away from your offices) is crucial since it helps everyone get away from the day-to-day and focus on working on the business.

Appoint someone on the team to lead the conversations just like Alan did. Take notes, have great discussions, and let us know how we can help you along the way.

Offsite Meeting 1

Chapters: Foundation Building – Meeting Cadence

Tools: Delegation Matrix, Roles & Responsibilities Chart, SMART Goals, Scoreboard, Weekly Meeting Agenda

Offsite Meeting 2

Chapters: Core Values – Grand Horizons

Tools: Core Values, Culture Check, 4 Strike Process (PIP)

Offsite Meeting 3

Chapters: Strategic Vision Page – The Back Page

Tools: Strategic Vision Page, The Framework Rollout Plan

Part One:
The Backstory

Christopher Reynolds

"Maybe I'm just not cut out for this."

It was hard to tell whether he said it aloud or thought it in his head. Looking at the clock, the green numbers glowed back at him: 2:37 AM. His wife rolled over, irritated that he woke her up again. It was too early to get up, so Chris just lay there, looking at the ceiling.

"How did I get here?" he thought to himself. He had recently been given an award for being an up-and-coming businessman in the area. While Chris accepted the award graciously, he couldn't help but feel like someone made a mistake.

Chris wasn't your typical businessman. He came from a small town in 'the middle of nowhere.' Some might say that was to his advantage. He worked on a small ranch in high school and knew how to buck bales and fix tractors.

He went to college like he was 'supposed to,' but he quickly found out after graduating that while a degree in medieval history might have been fun, it sure doesn't pay that well!

Chris began working in construction to put himself through school. He found that he had a knack for installing HVAC systems. With no real prospects of using his medieval history degree in a 'real job,' he kept working in construction and would do HVAC jobs on the side. Before he knew it, he was so busy that the side jobs became his full-time job.

Reynolds Industries quickly grew as Chris earned a reputation for getting the job done when he said he would. No one else in the area was as meticulous on the job or cared more deeply about the project than Chris.

After a while, Chris hired a few people, thinking it would free up his time. It's not that Chris didn't like the work; he could outwork just about anyone on the job site. That was his blessing and his curse.

He soon found out that hiring people just increased his responsibilities. This brought a whole separate set of problems that he never had before. Two steps forward, three steps back, it seemed... He didn't set out to be a 'business guy.' The faster the company grew, the more he felt behind.

"Are you going to call Alan tomorrow, or just keep talking to yourself all night?" his wife asked.

"Sorry, was I talking out loud."

"Mm-hmm..."

Chris knew something had to change. And while he hadn't talked to Alan in several years, Chris called him the following day, asking if he could visit. It was a rare window between busy seasons, and he knew he needed to take a breather and get some perspective.

On the way to Oregon, Chris hoped and prayed that Alan might have something for him.

Alan Mitchell

People may not have known Alan's name, but the evidence of his work was everywhere. There were business associations he had started that grew state-wide in three different states throughout his career. So many of the top companies in the towns he lived in were flourishing due to his influence.

Alan was a serial entrepreneur and couldn't help but grow companies. He had an incredible career as a businessman. His portfolio included everything from high-tech software systems to janitorial services. He even rang the opening bell at the New York Stock Exchange when a company he led was taken public.

Alan Mitchell was a geologist by education. He could see potential everywhere, unearthing precious metals in places where everyone else just saw rocks and dirt. Alan could see the potential 'gold' in business while others couldn't.

His 'secret' came from understanding people. He would always ask the big questions about why people do what they do. He understood human dynamics in a way that seemed almost 'spooky.'

This love for people is the reason his portfolio was so diverse. He constantly encouraged people to go into business and would often be the first investor to help get them started.

Alan, a devout family man, had four kids who thought the world of him. His wife was his biggest support and cheerleader, even when she didn't see the potential that Alan did.

Three of his kids followed in his footsteps as entrepreneurs. This chapter of Alan's life was helping his kids build their own companies. Alan now lived a few states away, working with his son, Tim, who was building a circuit board manufacturing company.

A 'great' company to Alan made an impact in the communities and lives that it touched. "Happy employees make happy customers," he would always say. *How* to do that requires a system and structure to build a company.

Alan and Chris met at church, where they both served on the 'Greeter Team.' The Greeter Team stood out in the snow, rain, and sun to welcome people to church. That was Alan, willing to serve wherever he saw the need.

It was Alan who encouraged Chris to go into business for himself all those years ago. Alan would periodically check in and see how Chris was doing, give tidbits of wisdom here and there as he was asked, but never impose himself.

Alan was excited to hear Chris's voice over the phone and could hardly wait to see Chris and discover what potential gold mine lay ahead.

The Visit

"I just don't know if I can keep going like this." Chris said, lounging on a couch in Alan's office, looking overwhelmed, "How do you do it?"

"Do what, exactly?" Alan replied empathetically.

"This. How are you able to run a company without losing your mind? Tim doesn't appear as stressed out as I am." Chris said, leaning back and looking out the window.

"Well," Alan said, "he probably isn't as stressed out."

"But HOW?"

"What is keeping you up at night, Chris?"

"It feels like everything right now. The guys are overloaded with work and feeling burnt out. And I don't know if we have enough money to hire more guys. A couple of the guys have constant bad attitudes, making me hesitant to hire more."

"What work are you doing these days?" Alan asked, "What does a typical day look like?"

"My phone is always ringing for one thing. If it isn't a customer, someone on the team asks me about something. I usually run around making bids and calling people back. Then once the day ends, I have a pile of paperwork to finish to send out invoices...."

Just then, Chris's phone rang as if on cue.

"See?" Chris said, silencing his phone.

"Who is responsible for handling sales calls?"

"Me."

"And who is responsible for ensuring the work gets scheduled and finished correctly."

"Me."

"And who is responsible for making sure invoices get sent out?"

"Me."

"Sounds like we have figured out the common denominator, at least." Alan laughed.

"That's why I'm here!" Chris said, exasperated.

"Chris," Alan said with a caring look on his face. "You're maxed out."

"I know that, but how do I fix it?"

"Let's start with something I call the three S's: Structure, Systems, and Strategy. Right now, it sounds like the 'structure' is that everyone reports to you, am I right?"

"That's true."

"And you don't have a system to run your company from; you're flying by the seat of your pants?"

"Also, true."

"And you don't have any overarching strategy you're using to help guide decisions?"

"Yep. We are unstructured with no system or strategy."

"Let's fix it then!" Alan said, excited.

"You make it sound too easy," Chris replied.

"Overnight success usually takes a few years."

"Well, whatever you're doing, I need to figure it out."

"It won't be as simple as flipping a switch, but I'll help you with the three S's if you're game."

"You'd want to come help?"

"I'd love to. We all need help. You probably like to 'do it yourself' for most things, but business is a team sport. The first step is to create a leadership team to come alongside and help you build the structures, systems, and strategy you need."

When Chris arrived home, he couldn't wait to tell his wife all about Alan's ideas. More than that, he could hardly wait for Alan to come and help get his team on track.

He started talking with people in the company that he thought could be part of this leadership team Alan would help him build.

Some team members pushed back as they couldn't see how so many people taking an entire day off work would be a good idea, especially with how far behind they were.

Chris trusted Alan and knew there had to be some changes if Reynolds Industries would continue to grow. As the leadership team started coming together, all Chris could ask them was to extend their trust in him to Alan.

Foundation Building

A few weeks later, Alan found himself in a small conference room several states away. Alan leaned against the conference room table, his gaze sweeping the assembled team. The room hummed with anticipation, a mix of curiosity and skepticism. Amanda, Luke, and a handful of others sat in mismatched chairs, their expressions ranging from apprehension to mild interest.

"I'm guessing you're all wondering who I am and why I'm here." Alan mused aloud.

"Pretty sure you're the guru Chris has been telling us about." Amanda replied, "And you're probably going to make us hold hands, do some trust falls or something like that."

Amanda Carter was brand new to the team. Although her background was working in a larger corporate structure, this was her first time working for a small company. She hoped to make an impact and have more say in her future rather than the constant fear of downsizing that plagued her career.

"Not exactly!" Alan smiled. "If you all want to do that, I'm not opposed, but that's not why I'm here."

"Why are you here then?" Daniel asked bluntly.

Daniel Timmons had been with Reynolds Industries for just six months. He was the best-dressed person in the room, with an outgoing personality and a flair for life. When you're someone like Daniel, you don't need to tell anyone you're cool... you just are. Never afraid to speak up, Daniel could also come across as very blunt. He always had a smile on his face... but he was blunt.

"I'm here for Chris." Alan responded, "At the end of the day, this is his company, and my goal here is two-fold. Number 1, we will create the structure and habits necessary for a company to grow. Number 2, we will create a leadership team to catalyze a healthy culture. With the right structure, habits, and culture, Reynolds Industries will be a fine-tuned machine."

"I think we're doing okay as it is." Luke protested, "I mean, no offense. I've been with Chris since almost the beginning, and we keep growing."

"But we can't keep growing this way," Chris interjected.

Luke Phillips was one of those 'salt of the earth' people. He was kind, generous, and always willing to help. Luke was a hard worker who took pride in his work and was passionate about being a family man. He always made sure that his family took priority over everything else outside of work.

"You've done a great job, Chris," Luke continued, "That's all I was trying to say. I have noticed you've been a bit more stressed lately... I just don't like change, that's all."

"Change can be hard," Alan said, stepping in, "and we can either accept the change or lead the change, but change is going to happen either way."

"Well said," Daniel replied, "So what are we doing?"

"First things first," Alan began, "we need to cultivate the right mindset in this room. Leadership isn't just about authority; it's about influence. Our outcomes won't align with our vision if we perpetuate the wrong mindset and attitude. Today, we're not merely employees working 'in' the business; we're the company's board of directors, collaboratively shaping its future."

"So, we can have our secret meeting and tell the team what they have to do?" Amanda asked. "Because I was one of those underlings in my last job for years, and it did not go over well."

"Let me start from the top, then," Alan said calmly, walking over to the whiteboard.

"Chris may have told you about my different successes over the years. And while those may be true, let me tell you about one of my biggest failures... The first company I was asked to run was manufacturing a new technology prototype. Think of your traditional 'start-up.' We had a little money, a good idea, and a few people invested in us. I didn't invent the technology or even understand manufacturing, but the two founders saw that I was good with people and asked me to be the CEO. The investments dried up, the manufacturing was taking longer than anticipated, cost way more than projected, and our product was unreliable."

"That sounds like a tough spot." Daniel said, "Did you turn it around?"

"No, I was fired." Alan said, "Instead of stepping back and creating the systems and structures I needed, I just worked more hours. We had to let people go during those eighteen months, and I picked up more and more responsibilities when those people left. I worked sixteen hours a day, sometimes seven days a week."

"That doesn't seem fair." Amanda said, "If you didn't invent the product, how were you responsible for it not working out?"

"There is a book I recommend to everyone called *Extreme Ownership*. Cliff notes: *Extreme Ownership* means taking full responsibility for everything within our purview— successes, failures, and missteps. Since I was the CEO, it was ultimately on me, and I failed."

"Did the company go under?" Daniel asked.

"No, they had another CEO step in, and that company is doing great things today and is worth nearly $500 million."

"Ouch," Amanda replied.

"It was an invaluable lesson. After a few weeks of licking my wounds, doing some soul-searching, and reflecting, I found that there are four fundamental areas that a company needs to focus on continually. And the thing that holds them together is the Vision."

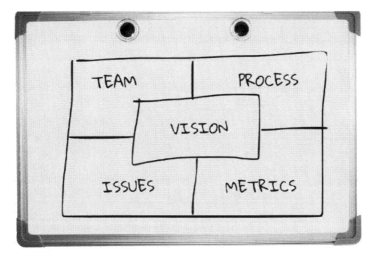

"Vision answers the questions, 'Why are we here?' and 'Where are we going?' It informs how we build our Team, 'who are we?', our Process, 'what do we do?', Metrics, 'how do we measure?', and Issues 'how do we handle issues that will inevitably come up?'"

"Sounds easy enough." Daniel said confidently, "We can wrap this up before lunch."

"Simple," Alan replied, "but not easy. This is the first of three meetings we will do over the next ninety days to set the course for Reynolds Industries in the next ten years."

"No pressure," Amanda said with a laugh.

"Will we all be here in the next ten years?" Ted asked.

Ted Jones was by far the quietest one in the room. He had an intense aura about him. One that inspired confidence in people. His team would follow him anywhere, and he rarely had to say a word. Ted had been with Chris the longest. Chris hired him six months after starting his company, needing someone he could rely entirely upon.

"Regardless of whether anyone in this room is here in the next ten years, we are the ones at the table today, and it is up to us to start setting the course."

Roles & Responsibilities

"First order of business, let's imagine that none of us in this room works for Reynolds Industries."

"So, we're all fired?" Daniel asked, smiling, "This will be a short meeting."

"I'm sure that everyone will be rehired by the time this meeting concludes today. "Alan responded, smiling back, "I say that because I've observed a common issue in many teams: a lack of clear roles and responsibilities. People step on each other's toes, or critical work falls through the cracks because people are not sure who is responsible for what."

"Today, as the 'board of directors,' it's our task to define the company's structure and identify the right individuals to fill those roles. You've likely seen organizational charts before, but ours won't be a typical organizational chart — we are creating a roles and responsibilities chart or the R&R Chart. We'll determine who is accountable for driving the company forward and in what ways."

"What does your current organizational structure look like?" Alan asked.

Chris answered, "It looks like I'm at the center of a bicycle wheel, with everyone coming to me for everything."

"How is that working?" Alan pressed.

"Not great," Chris admitted, "That was one of the main reasons I visited you a couple of months ago."

"One of the things we discussed, as you may recall," Alan added. "Is what I call 'CEO-itis' — where the owner becomes the go-to person for everything. This is a common pitfall. It's neither scalable nor sustainable."

"Where do we begin, then?" Amanda asked, "How do we figure out who to go to when Chris knows all the answers?"

"We'll start by focusing on the core functions or roles," Alan replied. "Every company has three main functions: someone who makes promises to customers, let's call it 'Sales,' someone who fulfills those promises 'Ops,' and someone who makes sure you don't go broke, 'Finance.' Let's build from there."

As Alan drew three circles on the board, he noticed nods of understanding around the room.

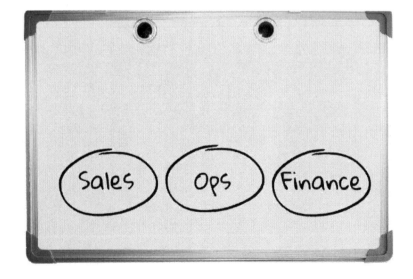

"The individuals who make promises are the growth engine of the organization. They identify problems and devise solutions. Once 'Sales' commits to a customer, it becomes 'Ops' responsibility to ensure that promise is fulfilled, while 'Finance' manages the cash flow. The final role oversees all three functions, harmonizing them for smooth operation."

"When Chris started this company," Alan continued, "he had to wear all the hats and be in every role."

"It made communication easier." Chris interjected, "They were quick conversations with myself about what I needed to do, and they got done."

"Absolutely." Alan agreed, "And the more people you add to the team, the more complex the communication channels become. The R&R Chart will help that."

Raising his hand, Luke asked, "What if there are more divisions or locations? Do we need multiple 'Ops' functions on the chart? We have guys that do maintenance and new construction and some that do both."

"It varies," Alan replied. "For this company, Luke, having two distinct operational functions might warrant adding a fourth person to the chart."

Drawing the fourth circle on the board, Alan asked the team, "Does this make sense so far?" Alan asked, receiving more nods. "Excellent. Now, let's outline the primary responsibilities for each function. For instance, what does 'Sales' do?"

"Sales handles finding new customers, creating quotes, and managing customer communication." Daniel said confidently, "That's what I do anyway."

"Structure first, then people." Alan reminded him, "And I agree with that role summary. Let's complete the rest of the responsibilities for the rest of the roles."

The chart was completed after discussing additional responsibilities and deciding on names for each role, including the CEO.

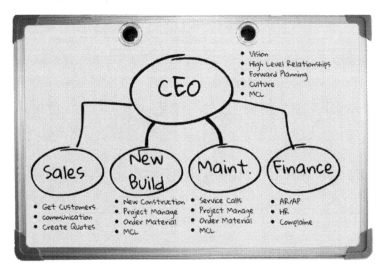

"Now that we've established the top-level structure," Alan continued, "we need key people to make up the Leadership Team. This team's job is to set the vision and maintain the culture to propel the company forward. Since you were all 'fired' earlier today, any nominations for who should lead this endeavor as the CEO?"

"Chris," the team chimed in unison.

"Makes sense, but before we volunteer him," Alan asked, looking over at Chris, "now that you understand the responsibilities, are you willing to take this on?" Alan asked.

"Sure." Chris responded hesitantly, "I'm not sure anyone else wants that headache."

"It's certainly much responsibility," Alan acknowledged, "But the goal is that it will be less of a headache, not more."

With Chris's name in the CEO role, the group swiftly assigned the 'Sales,' 'Finance,' and 'Maintenance' functions to Daniel, Amanda, and Ted, respectively. When Alan reached the 'New Build' role, Luke received a nomination.

"Hold on," Chris interjected. "Luke, you've been with me since almost the beginning. But considering the responsibilities, do you feel comfortable in this role?"

"Sort of?" Luke admitted sheepishly. "I like the work, but lining people out and dealing with demanding customers isn't my strong suit."

"Is it something you could learn or would rather not do?" Chris probed.

"It's not my personality," Luke agreed. "I'll do it and help wherever I'm needed, but every time I've been in charge of a project, it hasn't gone well."

"I've noticed that when Luke leads a job, it takes longer and consumes Chris's time." Amanda said, "Probably more time than if Chris did it himself. No offense, Luke."

"It's a fair assessment," Luke conceded. "I want to excel, but I don't think I should be in charge. Is that okay?"

"More than okay," Alan confirmed. "Delegation works when there's clarity about the task and ensuring the person you are delegating to has the ability, desire, and capacity. If any of those elements are missing, delegation can become a liability — a bigger headache than just doing it yourself. It's another common pitfall people encounter."

"But if Luke isn't the right fit for the role," Chris mused, "who will take it on?"

"You will," Alan replied. "Unless you have someone else in mind with the ability, desire, and capacity?"

"No one on the team that I can think of," Chris admitted. "But I'm swamped right now!"

"Well," Amanda said. "Functionally, you're already in the role. Rather than lie to ourselves, we should write your name in."

"The best part," Alan continued, "is that this highlights where your next hire should be. Your time needs to be freed up for other critical aspects of the company, namely being CEO."

With that, Alan penned Chris's name into the 'New Build' Seat, completing the top level of the chart.

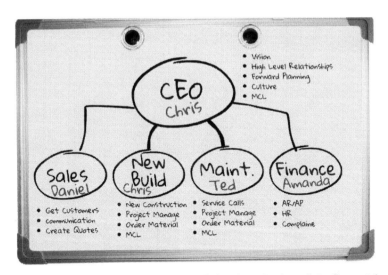

"I guess that explains some of the headaches," Luke said sheepishly, "sorry about that, Chris."

"Not your fault," Chris replied, slapping Luke on the back, "I did it to myself; you're one of the best guys I've ever been able to work with!"

"Learning how to lead a team isn't something that just happens." Alan interjected, "This is probably the best time to teach everyone what the 'MCL' means on the chart."

Mentor | Coach | Lead

"Each role on the chart needs five or fewer high-level responsibilities." Alan continued, "And if you have direct reports, one of the five needs to be MCL, Mentor, Coach, Lead."

"Isn't that just management?" Amanda asked.

"Management has a lot to do with ensuring the tasks get accomplished. I want to challenge you to think bigger than the task and focus more on the person doing the task."

Walking back to the table, Alan set down the marker. "Let me start by helping define what these words mean and how they relate. A mentor is someone who pours into a person; they give advice, teach, and develop. A coach is someone who draws the best out of a person. They see what is inside and what that person is capable of, which helps them win. A leader sets the direction and rallies people to move toward that goal. The focus is on the person, not on the task."

"Why does it matter?" Amanda asked, "If we pay people to do a job, shouldn't they just do it?"

"Next time we meet, we will dive into the intricacies of being fit for the team and whether people have the competencies for a job." Alan replied, "Today, I want to introduce the idea that I believe companies need less of a management team and more of a coaching staff."

"I played sports growing up," Amanda answered, "I think I see where you are going."

"If you are just a manager, you're inspecting to see if something was done. I'm sure you've all heard the term 'micro-managing,' but have you ever heard of 'micro-coaching'? If this company was a sports team and you were the coaching staff, what is the most important thing you need to know?"

"We need to know our players' strengths and weaknesses and the best position for them on the field, " Chris said.

"Exactly. I heard a remarkable story about John Wooden, who coached the UCLA Bruins basketball team in the 1960s and 1970s." Alan continued, "Legend has it that he would simply watch his players for the first several practices. After some time, he would go to a player and tell them he noticed specific spots on the court where that player would make most of their shots. Once he knew where they were most effective, he would design plays to put specific players in the exact spot he identified."

"They were a force to be reckoned with." Daniel added, "If that legend is true, it makes sense why they won so many games."

"The point I want to illustrate is that I want to encourage you to change your mindset from 'managing' to mentoring and coaching. You're a coach if you are responsible for caring for people on the team. And your position as a coach means pouring into your players and drawing the best out of them — casting vision for them about what winning looks like. Teach them how to do a move they have never seen before. Encourage them to be more than they think they can be because you see potential inside them that they don't see themselves."

"Which part is mentoring, coaching, and leading, then?" Scott asked.

"All the pieces work together in unison. The best coach I ever had in high school would do all three, depending on what I needed. Sometimes, I needed to believe that we, as a team, could win the championship. Sometimes, I needed the vision to see that I could be a starting player on that team. Those are leadership skills: vision, direction, and motivation. At other times, I needed help with my shot mechanics or making my passes less obvious. These I would call mentoring; he was pouring into me and teaching me things I didn't know before. And sometimes, I just needed him to kick my butt and let me know that I was capable of stopping being lazy and becoming better. I'd say that is the coaching aspect."

"Really," Chris interjected, "these are all different aspects of being a coach."

"Agreed. The reason I differentiate is to help bring language to the nuances of what a coach does, which is all three, in my opinion." Alan responded.

"And with any coach I had," Amanda added, "they had particular things that I needed to do to get better and be part of the team."

"Good point." Alan replied, "And let me ask you, Amanda, which teams did you perceive to be of higher caliber, ones that you could walk on or ones that you had to try out for?"

"Tryouts for sure." She responded.

"Similarly, I would propose that when you look at hiring people, you take the same approach. This isn't a pickup game you're playing; people need to try out for the team and prove to you that they have what it takes."

"This is a great way to look at it." Chris added, "I wonder what kind of team we would have today if I had that mindset."

"Bringing it back to the Roles and Responsibilities Chart, you also look for bench depth as a coach. Who on your team could move up in the organization as it grows, or could someone move on? I hope that by using the lens of coaching, you better understand how to create a team."

"How do we become better coaches then?" Chris asked.

"We will continue to work through that exact question, Chris." Alan responded, "The work we are doing today is a great first step. Now that we have the top level of the Roles and Responsibilities Chart, each person with direct reports needs to create the next levels down in their team. Let's make that a To-Do for Chris and Ted before we meet next time and take a break – that was a lot!"

Goals

"Now that we know who is responsible for what, let's talk about what needs to be done in the next 90 days," Alan said.

"That's a little vague," Daniel responded. "What do you mean? Like, what are we working on right now?

"What I mean," Alan replied, "is identifying the big important tasks that need attention but aren't screaming at you right now. The challenge with important matters is that they don't always demand immediate attention like urgent tasks. Here is a tool called the 'Eisenhower Matrix,' let me illustrate."

Back at the whiteboard, Alan drew four quadrants.

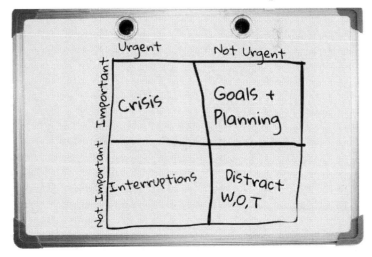

"Important, Urgent. Non-Important, Non-Urgent," he explained. "Most of our time gets consumed by urgent matters, whether truly important or not. Well-known author Stephen Covey calls this constant firefighting the 'whirlwind.' But how many of those urgent things are genuinely important? And if they are essential, do they align with your responsibilities?"

"Like toilet paper," Chris grinned.

"Um…. yeah," Amanda agreed, slightly embarrassed.

"I must have missed something," Alan admitted.

"Last week," Amanda said, "I came into Chris's office while he was working on a bid with Daniel. I asked him which toilet paper we should get because the one we've been using is more expensive, and we were about out."

Amanda chuckled, still a bit flushed.

Chris continued, "I told her it didn't matter as long as we had something other than leaves."

Alan burst into laughter. "That's exactly what I mean! The decision may be urgent, but Chris does not need to make that urgent decision. Now that we've clearly defined responsibilities, it's urgent and important for Amanda, who was responsible for office administration."

"But it would be non-important and non-urgent for the CEO," Chris said, smiling. "Unless we were completely out."

"Exactly," Alan confirmed. "With the Roles and Responsibilities Chart in place, Chris isn't handling toilet paper logistics. He does know whom to talk to, so we don't run out, though!"

"This doesn't solve your first question," Luke interjected.

"True. The toilet paper emergency addresses the distinction between urgent and non-urgent based on responsibility, but not the important versus urgent aspect," Alan replied. "Considering the responsibilities each of you have on the Roles and Responsibilities Chart, can you think of tasks that are important but not part of your daily routine?"

"Could you give us an example?" Chris inquired.

"Of course," Alan responded. "During the break, you mentioned running out of space for equipment at your current shop. Given your growth trajectory, will everything and everyone fit in your current space in a few years?"

"No way!" Luke exclaimed. "We're already bursting at the seams!"

"That is a good example of something important but not urgent," Alan explained. "It won't make or break you today, but if you don't direct some energy and intention toward it, you'll be in a tough spot a few years from now."

"And since part of my responsibilities involves forecasting and maintaining organizational health," Chris added, "it's on me to figure this out."

"You don't have to tackle it alone," Alan said, nodding in agreement, "but based on your responsibilities, focusing on this prevents it from becoming urgent. Forecast, plan, and look ahead."

"That's a good example," Amanda said, "but building a new shop won't happen in the next 90 days."

"Fair." Alan replied, "That may be a good one — or three-year goal, but the concept stays the same."

"I understand," Luke said. "We need to prioritize the important tasks that directly impact our part of the company."

After a brief discussion, Alan directed the team to write down the most crucial actions needed to propel the company forward in the next 90 days. Alan then compiled everyone's lists on the whiteboard.

"There's no way we can accomplish all of this in the next 90 days," Amanda observed. "Some of these items are more personal, not critical for the whole company."

"Great observation, Amanda!" Alan praised. Some are personal To-Dos, goals, or part of your day-to-day work. Now that we have the list, though, which ones are vital to moving the company forward?"

Leading the discussion, Alan went through the list, having the team combine themes, move some of the list to personal To-Dos for team members, and remove some items that would not be prioritized in the next 90 days.

"With these three main items left," Alan continued, "We need to ensure that these are SMART Goals."

"Insulting our intelligence now?" Daniel said, grinning.

"No." Amanda corrected him, "SMART is an acronym for how to set goals. I don't remember what each letter stands for, though."

"Happy to help." Alan interjected, "SMART is an acronym. Nice work, Amanda. 'S' stands for 'Specific.' What *exactly* do we want to have accomplished? 'M' stands for 'Measurable.' How do we measure and know that it *has* been accomplished? 'A' stands for 'Achievable.' What is your *plan* to accomplish the goal? 'R' stands for 'Relevant.' Why does this goal matter, and how does it help the business and its objectives? Finally, 'T' stands for 'Timely' or 'Time Bound.' When are you going to accomplish this goal? Let's put these things through that lens to clarify what we want to achieve.

After some discussion and debate, the team set the three priorities worded as SMART goals:

1) Create marketing binders to use during sales calls.

2) Implement a new phone system.

3) Purchase a new truck and trailer for a third crew.

"Now that we have these SMART goals," Alan continued, "who owns it? One person needs to be responsible for making it happen and report on progress weekly to the rest of the leadership team." He glanced at the Roles and Responsibilities Chart and helped the team see which team member owned each objective.

"The next step," Alan said, "is defining milestones."

He erased the board and began asking questions about the first objective.

"What do we need for these marketing binders?" Alan inquired.

Amanda responded without taking a breath, listing all the necessary components: "Pictures from the field, service descriptions, rough pricing, professional layout, organization, printing, and copies for Chris and Daniel to take on sales calls."

Alan struggled to keep up as he wrote it all on the whiteboard. "Is that everything?" he joked.

"Well," Amanda hesitated, "we also need to —"

Chris interrupted, "I think we get the high level."

"Agreed," Alan said. "Now, when will you complete all these tasks?"

"In the next 90 days," Daniel stated matter-of-factly.

"Exactly," Alan grinned. "But remember, each step is crucial to achieving our goal. Let's work backward from the end date to create milestones and stay on track."

Back at the whiteboard, Alan began putting dates to the tasks that the team had formulated.

"Amanda," Alan asked, "if this order is correct, when should we have these binders ready for sales calls?"

"By the end of April at the latest," Amanda replied.

"Okay," Alan continued, "when must they be printed?"

"April 25th," Amanda confirmed.

Alan helped Amanda set milestones for completing each task, ensuring they wouldn't hinder other necessary work.

"Does this all make sense?" Alan asked. "See how we created milestones based on sub-tasks?"

"But do we have time for all this?" Daniel interrupted. "We have our 'day jobs' still."

"I propose you don't have time *not* to do them," Alan grinned.

"What do you mean?" Daniel asked.

"Remember," Alan explained, "prospective clients want to know your work, how it looks, and approximate costs. Investing time upfront saves time during sales calls."

"Exactly," Chris added. "Leaving something with them sets clear expectations."

"And it's important but not necessarily urgent," Alan agreed. "Prioritize now to free up future time."

"As a leadership team," Alan continued, "if this goal falls behind, others can step in to keep it on track."

"How will we know if someone isn't on track with the assigned goal?" Chris asked.

"We'll cover that in our Meeting Cadence discussion," Alan replied. "Let's set milestones for the other two goals and then grab lunch — it just arrived!"

Metrics

"Before we dive into Metrics," Alan began, "I know that after lunch, when everyone's well-fed, it's tempting to take a nap. So, to kick things off, after our coaching discussion earlier, I'm curious which of you played sports as a kid?"

The following 10 minutes buzzed with everyone sharing their "glory days" of playing sports. Luke played baseball until high school, and Ted played rugby and ran track. Chris played football through high school, and Daniel played in a punk rock band. Everyone was the most surprised to learn that Amanda had been an NCAA Division I soccer star. No one believed her until Daniel did an internet search and discovered she was in the hall of fame at the university she attended.

Alan brought the conversation full circle, "In higher-level competition, how do you determine if a team is improving or declining?"

"Stats," Daniel confidently declared. "I love stats! I'm in several fantasy football leagues, and let me tell you, stats are everything."

"Exactly," Alan agreed. "In the business game, you also need stats and metrics to gauge whether you're on track or veering off course. My high school basketball coach obsessed over stats. While my 3-point percentage was decent — around 38% — I'll admit my free-throw percentage wasn't much better, hovering around 43%."

"That's pretty bad!" Daniel scoffed. "Even if you don't know basketball, that's pretty bad."

"True," Alan acknowledged. "And those stats revealed I needed to work on my free throws."

Chris said, "So, how do we translate sports stats to our business?"

"How do you know you're winning?" Alan replied. "I often see businesses measuring success solely by their bank balance — if it rose from last year, they're doing something right. But here's the catch: bank balance is a lagging indicator. If you're facing issues, you won't see them until year-end, and you could be in trouble by then. In sports, you look at the scoreboard during a game to assess where you stand and what adjustments are needed. Stats tell you how specific players are doing and how various aspects of the game are going. Offensive stats, defensive stats, etc. In business, we use metrics to give us that information, just like stats are used in sports."

"Of course!" Amanda interjected. "How else can we know if we're winning unless it's right in front of us all the time?"

"Exactly," Alan said. "Metrics show us key numbers week over week. Each metric will have a threshold, and if that threshold is breached, we know there's an issue to address."

Ted asked, "Could you explain thresholds a bit more?"

"Of course," Alan replied. "Thresholds should be set so you're alerted to a potential problem if broken. For instance, consider the metric 'Number of Leads.' If you typically have around ten leads per week, what would be a low number that raises concern?"

"Probably 8," Daniel replied, "If we have fewer than 8 in a week, it makes me nervous."

"Great!" Alan affirmed. "Let's set that threshold at 8. If we see seven or fewer leads, it signals a potential issue we must proactively address."

"If we revisit the Roles and Responsibilities Chart," Alan began, "each role should have key metrics informing us about the company's distinct aspects. For instance, the number of weekly leads gives insight into marketing performance. The success rate in winning jobs reflects the effectiveness of our sales process. And the time it takes to complete a job reveals operational efficiency..."

"Finance is all about numbers." Amanda interrupted, "No offense, but those should be straightforward."

"The crucial point," Alan emphasized, "is making these numbers visible to the entire team."

Chris hesitated. "But if everyone sees our numbers, won't that hurt us if someone leaves and joins a competitor?"

"I'm not suggesting we reveal our 'secret sauce,'" Alan clarified. "However, withholding information breeds uncertainty, leading to mistrust and chaos. While transparency's a small risk, the potential upside is enormous."

Unexpectedly, Ted spoke up. "I'd like to know how we're doing."

Chris looked surprised. "Ted, you've been with me the longest. You've seen most of the jobs and bids we've won."

"But that doesn't mean I understand our performance," Ted replied. "We're busier than ever, hiring like crazy, but I also know expenses add up when we invest in new equipment or face breakdowns. I 'think' we're okay, but I don't have a clear picture."

Alan affirmed, "And that's precisely why metrics matter. Running a company by the numbers—rather than 'flying by the seat of your pants'—is essential, Chris."

Chris seemed shocked. "I never thought about that. I guess I just assumed everyone knew how we were doing."

"Let's put some numbers on the board," Amanda stated confidently.

The team brainstormed key metrics they were responsible for and others they wanted to track. After consolidating ideas, they settled on a few critical metrics with thresholds:

Date	THRESH	RESP					
Leads	8	Daniel					
Jobs Won	35%	Daniel					
Job Loss	$500	Chris					
Service Call Time	60 min	Ted					
Cash on Hand	$250k	Amanda					

"Back to *Extreme Ownership*," Alan continued, "each metric must be assigned to an individual for weekly reporting. This ensures visibility and accountability across the company."

Luke raised a concern. "What if the numbers look bad? Do we fire people, or how does that work?"

"Metrics are indicators, not dictators." Alan explained reassuringly, "If certain numbers are off, it signals a potential issue that needs discussion. I read once that 'Numbers are not a substitute for leadership,' I could not agree more."

"Think of it like a car dashboard," Alan continued. "No warning lights? You're good. A green light on the numbers? No need to discuss. Yellow or red? Those become issues we address."

Ted grinned, speaking up again, "Sport and cars — things I can relate to. A dashboard warning light makes perfect sense."

41

"And these metrics aren't set in stone," Alan concluded. "We'll review them quarterly to ensure they align with our company's direction and growth targets."

"Ted's comment hit home," Chris interjected.

"What do you mean?" Alan asked.

"When he mentioned not knowing how we were truly doing," Chris explained, "I always had a vague sense of the numbers we needed to hit, but seeing them laid out like this on the Scoreboard is eye-opening."

"Now that I see it," Ted added, "it all makes sense. I'm not worried at all anymore."

"That makes two of us," Amanda chimed in. "While I handle the financial side, not having a clear picture of crew efficiency in the field has left me wondering if we'll keep up with the work or encounter unexpected challenges."

"Great feedback!" Alan encouraged. "Now that we've established the main components, let's integrate everything. All these pieces come together in the weekly meeting. The last agenda item for the day is the Meeting Cadence. This core habit will steer your company in the right direction and ensure everything stays on track. But first, I need to step outside for a quick walk — the beautiful weather is calling my name. Let's reconvene in 20 minutes."

Meeting Cadence

"Okay, folks," Alan began, his voice steady. "Before we dive in, let's get one thing straight: There are only two reasons you'd miss the weekly meeting. You're either on vacation or..." He paused, a hint of mischief in his eyes. "...you're dead."

Daniel, always the quick wit, grinned. "So, if you're not firing people, you're ensuring they aren't being killed off?"

Alan chuckled. "Something like that! But there's more. The other rule is simple: Start on time and end on time, every time."

Amanda shifted in her chair. "I'm not sure about this. We had weekly staff meetings at my last job, and we ALL hated them."

Alan nodded knowingly. "Ah, the classic 'death by meeting.' Let me guess. You all showed up with an agenda with bullet points for old and new business. Everyone talked in circles and shared opinions, but no real action items existed. It felt more like a whine-fest than accomplishing anything productive?"

Amanda nodded. "Yeah, that about sums it up. Sounds like you were in those meetings with us."

"Unfortunately," Alan admitted, "I've had my fair share of those meetings too. Allow me to propose something different. This meeting isn't about endless discussions. It's about results. Let me show you the agenda we use every week."

He strode over to the whiteboard and wrote the agenda:

Weekly Meeting Agenda:

Check-In	- 5 Minutes
Goals	- 5 Minutes
Metrics	- 5 Minutes
Headlines	- 5 Minutes
TODOs	- 5 Minutes
Issues	- 60 Minutes
Wrap-Up	- 5 Minutes

"Let me quickly explain all the pieces in order and why I believe the agenda is so critical," Alan began. "The purpose of the Check-In is to transition to 'being in' the meeting, hearing from everyone about what is happening in their work and personal lives. It's a beautiful place to celebrate wins within the team. You transition from working 'in' the business to working 'on' the business."

"Next, we have the Goals for the quarter. We've discussed these extensively, so we're all clear on them, right?"

Everyone nodded, so he continued.

"Rather than beating a dead horse, we set milestones to ensure that the Goals are either On or Off Track. This isn't a subjective feeling. It's not about sticking your finger in the wind. If you're hitting your milestones, you're On Track; if not, you're Off Track."

"What if we don't have milestones for a goal?" Luke asked.

"That's why we have to have milestones," Chris replied.

"Exactly," Alan agreed. "In this part of the meeting, we simply report whether a goal is On or Off Track. If it's On Track, discussing it further is unnecessary. If it's Off Track, it becomes an issue to address. We don't delve into the details here; we flag it as an issue and move on. Does that make sense?"

"It does," Amanda said. "I'm guessing that's why this section is only 5 minutes long."

"Yep!" Alan affirmed. "Each section—from Goals to To-Dos—is allocated 5 minutes to report the facts. We don't discuss; we consolidate everything into the Issues section, where we prioritize and tackle the issues based on priority."

Chris asked, "How do we prioritize?"

"We'll cover that in a moment," Alan replied. "But for now, let's quickly move through the next three sections."

"Similarly, with Metrics, we report on numbers that show where we stand as a company. Remember, just like the dashboard on a car. If the numbers look good, it's a green light—no need for discussion. If they're yellow or red, those become –"

"An issue that goes to the Issues list!" Daniel chimed in. "I think I'm getting the hang of it now."

Alan smiled and continued, "The next section covers Headlines. These are informational bulletins about customers, employees, events in other parts of the company, and employee time off. While these serve as heads-up notifications, anyone on the team who wants to discuss a specific item can add it to the issues list for a more in-depth conversation. The last section is the To-Dos list."

"I don't know if we can handle more To-Dos," Chris protested. "We're already swamped with tasks."

"The purpose of these To-Dos isn't to create more busywork," Alan explained. "They help you focus your effort and prioritize the most important tasks in your week. These To-Dos become high-priority tasks to move the team forward. Milestones for your Goals as To-Dos. As our leadership team solves issues, we'll identify To-Dos that address root problems, ultimately improving overall company operations."

"And for our To-Dos, do we simply report Done or Not Done?" Amanda asked. "Similar to how we handled our Goals?"

"Gold star for you, Amanda!" Alan said with a smile. "Exactly — no excuses, no lengthy discussions. Report if a To-Do is Done or Not Done. If it is done, give a quick synopsis of the outcome. If someone else on the team needs to know the resolution next steps or has a question, we –"

"Make it an issue," everyone said in unison.

"Correct," Alan affirmed. "Now that we've consolidated everything into the Issues List, it's time for the 'real work' of solving problems. Often, the issues list can be quite extensive, with potential duplicates. Before tackling it, we use a method I call 'Keep, Kill, Combine.' We read each issue aloud. If someone wants it to stay on the list, they say 'Keep.' If an issue has already been resolved and doesn't need discussion, anyone can say 'Kill.' In case of a debate, the tie goes to the runner—you keep the issue on the list. And duplicates are combined."

"Now that we have our condensed list, let's prioritize the Top 3 issues for discussion. Someone nominates an issue, and if there's no disagreement, it becomes numbers 1, 2, and 3."

"Is this where the 'real work' begins?" Daniel joked.

"Yes, sir," Alan replied. "Now we roll up our sleeves! Starting with issue number one, the person who added it to the list states the issue as clearly as possible. I follow the 3 R's for problem-solving: Realize, Root, Resolve. Like in every twelve-step program, the first step is admitting we have a problem—even though we might not like to admit it, we all have issues. Number 1, Realize."

"Well, we can't tackle all my issues here," Daniel laughed. "It'd take more than an hour!"

Everyone joined in the laughter, lightening the mood even further.

"Well, Daniel," Alan quipped, "we won't address all your issues today. However, being honest about the problems within the company is a positive step. We can't fix what we don't know about. Transparency encourages our teams to surface issues."

"Once we've realized the issue and stated it concisely, we need to dig into the root cause. Step one: Realize. Step two,

Root. Let me explain the 5 Whys method. You ask 'Why' five times to drill down to the root of an issue. Here's a good example," Alan said, writing on the board:

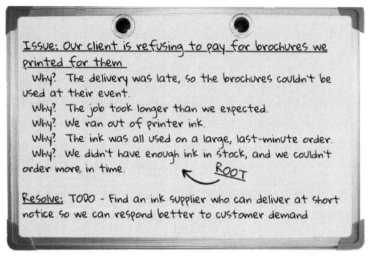

Issue: Our client is refusing to pay for brochures we printed for them
Why? The delivery was late, so the brochures couldn't be used at their event.
Why? The job took longer than we expected.
Why? We ran out of printer ink.
Why? The ink was all used on a large, last-minute order.
Why? We didn't have enough ink in stock, and we couldn't order more in time. ← ROOT

Resolve: TODO - Find an ink supplier who can deliver at short notice so we can respond better to customer demand

"We know we've found the root when we ask the 'why' question until we get to the root. This example is from my son Tim's company just last week. In this example, if we had a supplier who could deliver on short notice, would we have been able to meet the deadline and get paid?"

"That makes complete sense!" Amanda said excitedly. "Once you've figured it out and put it into a To-Do, this sort of thing shouldn't happen again. You identify what needs to be done so that discussions don't go in circles without progress."

"Exactly," Alan agreed. "While there will always be issues, this specific one shouldn't resurface. This is how the To-Dos flow back into next week's meeting. Assign the To-Do to the right person, and it holds everyone accountable for completing it by the following week."

"Now, we simply cross off the first issue and move on to the next. Once we've resolved those three, we nominate the next three. Most issues stem from either process problems or people problems. This is an example of a process problem," Alan said, pointing to the whiteboard. "People problems fall into three categories: lack of training, lack of skill, or not being a core values fit. While we won't tackle core values today, they're crucial for building a cohesive team."

"What if you run out of time before addressing all the issues on the list?" Chris asked.

"Most times, you won't get through the entire list," Alan explained. "Prioritization matters—you handle the most critical items first. Remember the 'start on time and end on time' rule? Be aware of the clock; you need the last 5 minutes of the meeting to Wrap Up. In these final minutes, we review the To-Dos everyone signed up for, then we rate the meeting, which gives the feedback needed to ensure that the meeting was productive and that we're moving forward as a team."

"Is this the same agenda for every meeting?" Daniel asked.

"Great question," Alan continued. The Meeting Cadence is a series of meetings. For now, we will focus on the Leadership Team Weekly Meeting. Once this meeting is mastered, every department will have its own Weekly Meeting."

"That's a lot of meetings," Daniel replied, concern in his voice.

"I didn't even get to the one-on-one meetings yet!" Alan said with a smile. "One-on-one meetings also happen weekly between a team leader and any direct reports they have. I would encourage you never to have too big of a span of control so that the number of meetings is manageable."

"Sounds like I'll always be in meetings." Chris interjected, "Why do we need so many meetings?"

"Mentor, Coach, Lead, right?" Alan responded, "So many problems in a company stem from poor communication. The purpose of the one-on-one meetings is to address issues in the team meetings; team meetings bring issues up in the leadership meetings. The goal is to solve an issue as far down in the organization as possible but ensure there is a way to escalate things routinely."

"It also allows for feedback to individuals on the team." Amanda added, "If I can get feedback and know when I have time to discuss issues with you, Chris, I won't bombard you with questions randomly throughout the day."

"The one-on-one meeting agenda is a bit more simplified than a weekly meeting agenda, but the principle is the same." Alan continued. "You look at metrics for that team member, review their goals and milestones, work through issues, and build rapport with them. It seems counterintuitive at times, but the entire meeting cadence moves the company forward faster by slowing down and taking the time to communicate effectively. This becomes especially important as the team grows."

"Sounds good to me," Chris said. "When's our first meeting?"

"Right now!" Alan replied. "Let's dive into the inaugural Leadership Team Meeting of Reynolds Industries!"

Core Values

"It's been about a month since we last met," Alan began, "So, how have the past few weeks been?"

"Well," Chris began, "the weekly meetings have been constructive. But they don't flow as easily as when you ran our first meeting last month."

"Great to hear that it's been helpful!" Alan responded. "It's true when you do anything new. When my kids were little, they were terrible at walking. I didn't give up on them and say, 'Well, looks like you'll just have to crawl forever.' The important part is that you're doing the meetings. New habits take time."

"It's been a bit rough, if I'm honest," Amanda interjected. "The leadership team meetings are going well, but we're getting resistance from some of the team."

"What do you mean?" Alan asked.

"Well," Amanda continued, "we came back super excited after our first meeting last month. A few of the guys just mocked it and wondered if we sat around singing kumbaya. One of the guys, Dylan, was almost hostile."

"Change is hard," Alan agreed, "especially for people who don't have a growth mindset."

"How do we instill that mindset in the team?" Chris asked.

"In my experience, you can't make anyone change. Some people want to change, and some don't. You can encourage, show, and provide resources but can't force a growth mindset into a team. You have to start by setting the right culture. Step one is to answer the question, 'What are our core values?'"

"See," Amanda interjected, "core values are the kind of kumbaya stuff the guys were worried about."

"I don't think it's kumbaya stuff, Amanda." Chris said, "I think we are setting a standard for the team to see if they have the same motivators we do."

"That's a good way to put it," Alan replied. "We'll return to Dylan and the others later, but let's talk about what core values are and are not."

Alan walked over to the whiteboard, drawing three concentric circles.

"I didn't come up with this," he stated. "This idea of the 'Core Values Traps' came from Patrick Lencioni. The first trap is aspirational—this isn't who we are but who we wish we were. We need to avoid this trap because if it isn't congruent with who we are, it makes us liars. The second trap is accidental—just because everyone at the company likes hiking doesn't mean that's a core value; it's more of a shared hobby. The third trap he calls 'permission to play'—these are one-word values that feel more like clichés: honesty, integrity, trust. Yes, people need to have integrity. You wouldn't hire someone you knew would steal from you, right? We want short phrases that are unique to you but carry deep meaning. These become the standard by which we promote, hire, and fire people."

"My head's already spinning," Chris remarked. "Where do we start?"

"I was getting there." Alan responded with a smile. "Let me start by asking the question: If you could clone one person in the company who isn't in the room, who would it be and why?"

"Luke," Amanda responded immediately.

"All right, why is that?" Alan asked.

"He's genuine, hard-working, and the guys like working with him."

"But wait," Chris interrupted, "Luke didn't make the cut, remember?"

"He didn't make the cut for the leadership team," Alan replied, "but that was about the responsibility of the role, not that he wasn't a culture fit. Let me ask another question: Where would your company be if you had ten Lukes working for you?"

"Holy smokes," Chris responded. "Yeah, we would be able to handle way more work and with way fewer headaches!"

"That makes Luke a perfect 'core values clone' then. Who else, not in this room, would you want to duplicate?" Alan asked.

"I'd take another Jake or two," Daniel grinned. "That guy can make the day fly by! No matter what we're doing, he always has a great attitude and makes the work fun, even when it sucks."

"He's not the fastest guy we have, but I agree," Amanda said.

After more discussion, the team identified a handful of characteristics they wrote down on the whiteboard from the 'clones' they identified.

"I see a few themes," Alan mused. "One thing that stands out right away is the theme of positivity, being a team player, and having a great attitude. The second major theme is a hard worker who figures things out. And the last theme is a person who goes above and beyond, doing more than just the minimum..."

Alan paused for a moment to let the team digest it all. "Thoughts?" he asked, breaking the silence.

"These look good," Chris started, "but how are these not clichés? We want a hard-working team player who does more than expected... isn't that what everyone wants?"

"You'd be surprised how many companies have never articulated even that," Alan said with a grin. "And you're right, we need to make these less clichés and add some meaning. When you say 'team player,' that means a lot of different things to different people. When you say 'positive,' you could be talking about someone who is unrealistically optimistic or overly nice but not honest with you."

"Or we could mean Jake," Amanda interjected. "That's what we want."

"Okay, how do we define that then?" Chris asked.

"When I think of Jake, I think of someone with an unrelenting good attitude regardless of the circumstances. He says all the time, 'I love it when it sucks!' with a big grin on his face that lifts everyone's spirits."

"Relentless Positivity Despite Adversity?" Alan inquired.

"That is a lot closer," Chris said thoughtfully. "Is that a short phrase that would be a core value?"

"It might be a little long, but it's sure a good place to start," Amanda agreed. "And it doesn't sound cliché; it sounds like you're describing Jake."

"Let's leave this one for now, then," Alan continued, "and let's work on the rest."

After another half hour or so of wordsmithing, the team came up with three core values they felt represented what they wanted to see in a teammate. They wrote them on the whiteboard:

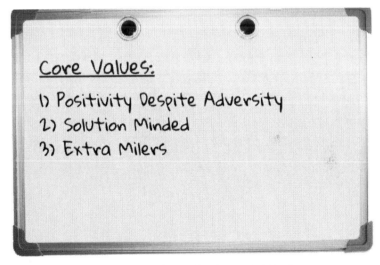

Core Values:

1) Positivity Despite Adversity
2) Solution Minded
3) Extra Milers

"How do these feel?" Alan asked inquisitively.

"I like them," Chris said with a nod. "I think they need to be explained a bit, though."

"I completely agree," Alan concurred. "This is why you're going to write a talk around the core values, what they mean, and specifically how you have seen them exemplified in the team using real-life examples. That's part of your homework as the CEO, Chris."

"Oh man, I hate public speaking," Chris said apprehensively.

"Let's not worry about that for now," Alan continued. "The next part of checking the core values is to make sure we aren't lying to ourselves; we exemplify and model the core values here on this team. If these core values aren't true for the leadership team, it would be better not to have any."

"Now we get to do the kumbaya stuff," Amanda said half-jokingly.

"It might be a bit more painful than that, I'm afraid," Alan countered. "And I need to ask everyone in the room's permission... can we be completely honest with each other during this exercise? This is not the time to hide feelings or pull punches; this is where trust happens."

"Kumbaya sounds like more fun."

Everyone in the room laughed at Scott, who finally broke his silence. The comment coming from him made it even funnier.

"It won't be too painful, I promise," Alan said reassuringly.

Culture Check

Back at the whiteboard, Alan drew a matrix with the core values listed above and the names of each leadership team member on the left.

"I call this tool the Culture Check," Alan began. "We're all going to get peer review feedback on how we're doing with these core values. Let's start with Chris."

"Uh-oh," Chris said, smiling. "You already fired me last time you were here, so why not?"

Alan continued, "We do this with a 'finger shoot.' Chris is in the hot seat, and I'll say the first core value, count to three, and on three, everyone gives a thumbs up, thumbs down, or thumbs to the side. Thumbs up means he exemplifies this core value most of the time. Thumbs down means he rarely does, and thumbs to the side means it's hit or miss."

"What if someone is the opposite, like a negative core value?" Amanda asked.

"I think there's a different finger for that," Scott said unexpectedly.

After the laughter subsided, Alan was glad to see Scott finally engaging in the conversation.

Scott Fitzpatrick was a new face at the offsite meeting. After the last meeting, conversations were swirling amongst the team about what Chris and the rest wanted to accomplish. Having only been on the team for three months, Scott felt he could be a good fit for heading up the New Build Role. After some conversation about the expectations for the role, Chris thought he could be the right fit and invited Scott to be part of this offsite meeting.

"Thanks for that insight, Scott," Alan said, still chuckling. "You can also see the other end of the Culture Check where I have Ability, Desire, and Capacity written. Another concept I learned from Jim Collins, who authored the book *Good to Great.* In the book, he describes getting the 'right people on the bus.' Our Core Values define these. If someone is a core values fit, they are the Right Person. I believe this is more important than qualifications. I hear it put once that you hire for attitude over aptitude."

"What if they don't know what they're doing though?" Amanda asked, "Some people just suck at their job."

"That is the other piece from Jim Collin's book. Once you have the right person on the bus, you must ensure they are in the right seat. We used Luke as a model to create the core values. He is the right person on the bus, but leading the new build team was not the right seat for him. We want the right people in the right seat, or the shorthand, RPRS."

"That's why you had us start with the Roles and Responsibilities Chart first," Chris stated. "When we know what is required in the role, we can see if someone would be good at it.

"I guess that's why I'm here," Scott replied. "I saw the role and what you needed and felt like I could help as it aligns with work I was doing before I moved here."

"And the fact that you brought me a four-page document outlining *how* you would do it helped." Chris quipped. "Your initiative blew me away."

"You're exactly right, Chris." Alan continued, "Core Values answer the right person's question. Ability, Desire, Capacity, or ADC answer the right seat question. Let me quickly define ADC so we are all on the same page. Ability is simply that: do they have the skills required to do the job; are they competent in the position? Desire is asking if they want the position. Many people can *do* a job, but do they want the job? Is the desire there? Capacity asks if they have the experience and resources to take on the work required for the role."

"What do you mean by Capacity?" Amanda asked inquisitively.

"Here is a good way to look at it." Alan began, "Let's say that every person is a container. Some people are a one-gallon jug, and others are fifty-gallon drums. If the position requires twenty gallons of work, a fifty-gallon capacity person can handle that with no problem. If they are a one-gallon capacity person, they will be overwhelmed."

"That makes sense." Chris replied, "Or if they are a fifty-gallon drum and already have forty gallons worth of work, they can't take on another twenty gallons."

"Great observation, Chris." Alan encouraged. "And keep in mind that people can expand their capacity. I believe that people expand their capacity largely based on experience. Things that used to take you all day when you first started probably take a fraction of the time now."

"Thanks for the clarification," Amanda said. "For the person to be right for the role, they need the ability to do the job, want the job, and can handle what the job requires."

"You got it!" Alan responded, "That is why you need the right person in the right seat. Wrong person, wrong seat; it's a drag to the team. Right person, wrong seat; you cause confusion because they fit the culture but suck at their job. If you have this situation, you can see if they have another seat on the bus. Don't make up a new seat, but do they have the ability, desire, and capacity to move into a new role?"

"Like Luke." Amanda said, "I get it now."

"If you have the wrong person in the right seat, you cause frustration. They may be good at the job, but they are sucking the soul out of the team."

"Kyle," Ted interjected. "People walk on eggshells around him, never knowing if he will blow a fuse. If we have the right people in the right seats, we can make this company incredible."

Ted speaking up that way carried more weight than if Alan had explained it. He didn't talk much, but when Ted spoke, everyone listened.

"Does everyone understand the finger shoot?" Alan asked, bringing the focus back to the whiteboard. "Let's start with Chris and core value number one: 'Positivity Despite Adversity.' Ready, 1... 2... 3... Shoot!"

Alan noted the average result from the finger shoot. Chris passed with flying colors, getting all thumbs-ups. It wasn't until they got to Amanda and core value number three that they saw the first thumbs down.

"Scott," Alan began, "Why a thumbs down for Amanda?"

"Well," Scott started hesitantly, "I know you do good work, Amanda. It's not an attack on that. It's just that when we get back from the field and have piles of paperwork, you wrap up what you're doing and head out early without asking if any of us need help. I know I'm pretty new to the team, and this is my first meeting, but it's just something I've noticed."

"I didn't know you wanted my help," Amanda said, somewhat annoyed. "I'd be happy to help if someone asked me."

"This is a good conversation to have," Alan mused. "First off, thank you for your courage to be honest, Scott. Trust can only happen in candid conversations that are uncomfortable. That said, on any team, it's easy to focus on your part and become oblivious to others needing help. That said, did you ever ask Amanda for help, Scott?"

"No," Scott admitted. "I was just hoping she would ask."

"I'm not a mind reader," Alan stated. "And I doubt Amanda is either. The takeaway is that to be a good teammate, we need to ask for help when needed. And if we have extra capacity, we need to ask how we can help. Good?"

Everyone nodded in agreement.

"Now, that said," Alan continued, "Scott, would you keep your thumbs-down assessment?"

"Given that perspective, no, it would be a thumb to the side," Scott responded.

"That's fair," Amanda said positively.

After the rest of the team had a chance to be in the hot seat, the Culture Check was filled in.

"Looking at this now," Alan began, "everyone on this team is a core values and culture fit. But no one is perfect. We need to establish the standard for being on the team. The leadership team standard seems to be two thumbs up and one neutral. What do you all feel the standard should be for everyone else?"

"Maybe a bit lower?" Chris asked hesitantly. "We are in a blue-collar industry, after all."

"I'd recommend no lower than one step," Alan replied. "You attract what you are. High standards attract high-standard people. Lower standards don't attract high-standard people, and you'll constantly deal with mediocre performance and attitudes because that's what you tolerate."

"You attract what you are. You get what you tolerate," Amanda repeated. "That makes a ton of sense."

"Then our employee standard should be at least one thumbs up and two neutrals," Scott said confidently.

"How do we all feel about that?" Alan asked.

"Don't you think that's a little high, though?" Chris replied. "We hire tons of entry-level jobs, and some of these guys have rough backgrounds."

"You attract what you are. You get what you tolerate," Amanda repeated. "We've probably kept several people too long in the past, and they have caused so many issues."

"All right," Chris responded. "As long as you all have my back on this, I'm good with it."

"Settled then," Alan continued. "The standard for the leadership team is two thumbs up, one neutral. The standard for the rest of the team is one thumbs up and two neutrals. Next, we will run the Culture Check for the rest of the team."

After listing the rest of the team on the whiteboard and going through the Culture Check, two names stood out, with thumbs down on core values and Desire.

"This makes it so clear," Chris said, leaning back in his chair. "How did we not see this before?"

"That's what makes this tool so powerful," Alan said. "It highlights what you already knew to be true, but in a way that pinpoints the issue that needs to be addressed."

"So, what do we do about Dylan and Kyle?" Amanda asked bluntly. "Do we call them today and tell them to pack their bags?"

"Not exactly," Alan replied. "All business is a people business, and we must do right by the people we lead. Since these core values are new, it wouldn't be right or fair to walk in tomorrow and let them go. The ripple effects on the rest of the team would be confusing and detrimental."

"Not to mention, we're short-staffed as it is," Scott mused. "We need them."

"Yes and no," Alan responded. "Yes, you're short-staffed. I've seen that on your issues list. But no, you don't sacrifice your team culture for one bad apple. If one person left today, you'd scramble for a bit, but the team would figure it out and move forward. That's reality."

"That seems like a contradiction," Amanda pondered. "You said we want to do right by them and not fire them today, but you're also saying we can let them go today and be fine. Which one is it?"

"Yes," Alan said, smiling. "Both are true. We don't tolerate people who aren't a culture fit. The way we do right by them is to communicate where we see the lack and put together a plan to mentor, coach, and lead them to be a core values fit."

"How do we do that?" Chris asked. "We've talked to Dylan and Kyle about their attitudes."

Walking back to the whiteboard, Alan continued, "Let me introduce you to something I call the '4 Strike Rule.'"

4 Strike Rule

Standing at the whiteboard, Alan continued, "Strike 0 is when you first have a concern that needs to be addressed as soon as possible. Let's use showing up late as an example; which core value does this highlight to you?"

"Extra Milers," Chris said confidently. "If you're not showing up on time, you're not likely to be the person putting in the extra effort."

"Exactly," Alan continued. "Strike 0 is just an informal conversation. Something like, 'Hey Kyle, I noticed you came in late today. Is everything okay? One of the things that makes this team special is that we are Extra Milers, meaning we always go above and beyond and pay attention to the little things. Being on time is one of those things, so I just wanted to make sure you were good. Is there something bigger, or should I not expect you to be late anymore?'"

"Oh, that's good!" Scott said excitedly. "It calls them out but is nice at the same time, and it communicates the standard."

"You got it!" Alan agreed. "And remember, all business is a people business. An informal conversation asking if everything is all right allows you to connect with them. Maybe they have a challenge you don't know about, or their car broke down. It's not about fishing for excuses but showing you care while making expectations clear."

"So, what's Strike 1?" Scott asked.

"Strike 1 is a more formal meeting where you address the specific concern and give the expected corrective action. Using the lateness example, you'd say, 'Kyle, we talked last week about you not being late. You were late again today, so let me clarify: we can't have you coming in late because it negatively affects the rest of the team.' After this conversation, you email them the bullet points and have them reply to confirm they understood."

"So, nothing in their file at this point?" Amanda asked.

"You can if you want, but the main thing is to get it in writing somewhere in case you need it in the future," Alan responded. "Hopefully, a formal conversation followed by an email will remedy it."

"So, Strike 2 goes in their file?" Scott inquired.

"Yes. Strike 2 is a meeting with three people: the employee, yourself, and one other member of the leadership team or HR. This reinforces the seriousness. You give the employee a written explanation of the problem and the expected corrective steps. The employee gets a copy and signs one for their file. This starts the official Performance Improvement Plan, or PIP, putting them on probation."

"How do they get off probation?" Chris asked. "Are they on it forever?"

"A good rule of thumb is that it's hard to get on a PIP and harder to get off," Alan acknowledged. "The PIP is reviewed weekly to ensure the employee is on track. Once on a PIP, the employee doesn't get off for six months. If they fix the problem and can sustain the change needed, you have a meeting to remove them from probation officially."

"Six months?!" Amanda said in disbelief. "We just let it drag on for six months?"

"No, the goal is that they correct the action, and it doesn't continue to be an issue. We're making sure they sustain the change for six months," Alan replied. "Anyone can correct something short-term, but six months shows true change. If they can't sustain the standard during those six months, they move to Strike 3."

"And then we let them go?" Chris inquired.

"Correct," Alan responded. "Strike 3 is a meeting with the same people as Strike 2. You give the employee a written document explaining that they haven't corrected the situation and are being terminated effective immediately."

"This sounds like it will take forever," Amanda said.

"In my experience," Alan replied, "people who reach Strike 2 usually self-select out. They don't like being under the microscope and will find another job, or they're not a core value fit and won't sustain the change needed."

"How long do you wait between Strike 0, Strike 1 and Strike 2?" Scott asked thoughtfully.

"It can happen as quickly as a week," Alan responded. It's up to the employee to change. Remember, as leaders, we want to mentor, coach, and lead people on our team. Your job is to clearly communicate the standard and see if there is a way you can coach or mentor them. The four-strike process ensures that no team member is shocked when someone is let go. The team understands that the process is fair and not arbitrary. "

"What about if someone is caught stealing or drunk driving with a company vehicle?" Scott asked.

"Those are blatant and obvious reasons that can have legal repercussions," Alan replied. "You can decide whether to take legal action, but they are fired immediately for cause. That should be obvious to the team. Of course, you document it and put it in their file."

"Core values, ability, desire, and capacity are more nuanced," Scott observed. "I like how the '4 Strike Rule' works; it seems fair."

"So," Amanda said more seriously, "what are the next steps for Dylan and Kyle?"

"Since you've already talked to them about their attitudes, Chris, that's already the Strike 0 conversation," Alan continued. "Next, have a conversation tying their bad attitude to a core value and how it hurts the team. Since you gave both of them a thumbs down for desire, I think your next conversation would be asking them if they want to be here. If they are miserable and making the team miserable, it may help open the dialogue. If they don't want to be there, help them find another company to land at. If they say they do want to be here, you need to have clear expectations of how their attitudes need to change. Then send them each an email with the bullet points and get them to reply that they understood it."

"Strike 1 conversation," Scott mused.

"Exactly," Alan said. "Amanda, can you please make that a To-Do for Chris, due by next week?"

"I see how the Weekly Meeting helps hold us accountable," Chris stated.

"What do you mean by that?" Alan asked.

"These are things I would have let slide before. But knowing I have to report back next week, I will get it done where before I wouldn't do it."

"We all need accountability," Alan responded. "There's a reason people have personal trainers; it's not because they don't know how to do push-ups!"

"Okay," Amanda responded, "I have those two To-Dos set for next week for you, Chris. What's next?"

"I think we all need a break!" Alan responded. "That was some heavy lifting. Let's take 20 minutes, get some fresh air, and then jump back in."

Define the Why

After the much-needed break, the team reassembled with renewed energy. The room was filled with laughter and chatter as Alan brought everyone's focus back to the day's priorities.

"Core Values: Check!" Alan said. "Part one of crafting the vision is complete. 'Who are we?' is the most important question we can answer. The second most important question is, 'Why do we do what we do?'"

"That's easy," Amanda began. "We're here to make money."

"There are plenty of ways to make money," Alan countered. "Why do you choose to do so here, at this company? Your original 'why' might have been just that; many on your team might have the same initial why. It's okay; we all need to make a living. But as a company, you don't exist *just* to make money. If that was the driver, there are ways to make money that might not be ethical or could be short-sighted."

"Why did you start the company then?" Scott asked, looking at Chris.

"To make money!" Chris said with a laugh. He continued, "I started because I was tired of working for someone else. It felt like so many dead-end jobs in construction. I was just a pair of hands. No one bothered to see if I had more potential. So, I showed up, did my work, went home, and got a paycheck. It was boring and unfulfilling. I started working for myself, treated people the way I wanted to be treated, and, yes, had to make money to make a living. Then, before I knew it, I had to hire people. Now it feels like my focus is ensuring that the people who work for us don't feel the same way I did..." Chris's voice trailed off.

"And?" Scott asked intently, leaning forward.

"Well, I guess that's why we're here," Chris stated. "I'm not sure if I'm living up to that ideal and taking care of people. I wonder how many people who work for us feel like I did — uninspired, unfulfilled, and bored."

"Let me ask you the same question, Scott," Alan said inquisitively. "Why are you here at this company? What attracted you?"

"Exactly what Chris said," Scott responded. "We've all had those dead-end jobs where it feels like we're running around like crazy, working hard, but not appreciated. I've only worked here for three months, but I can tell how genuine Chris is and how much he cares about this team."

"I appreciate that," Alan continued, "but that still didn't get to the heart of the question. Why are you working here, of all places?"

"To be part of the team and help create a great work environment," Scott responded. "Other people I've worked for don't care about people nearly as much as Chris does."

"I don't think this is what Alan means," Amanda responded. "It's not like we can put that on a billboard."

"I disagree," Alan replied. "I think we're onto something here."

Alan drew a giant bullseye on the whiteboard, labeling the three parts, starting at the center.

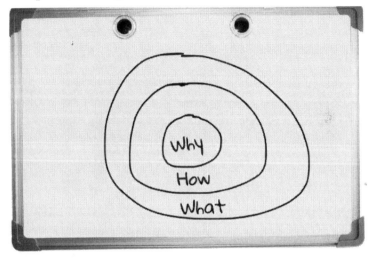

"I steal some of my best ideas!" Alan said with a wink. "This one I stole from Simon Sinek and his book, *Start with Why*. The main premise is when companies begin with 'What' they do, like construction, or 'How' they do it, like a proprietary method or process. Those are decent marketing points but aren't the intrinsic driver behind human motivation. In your case, people don't work for you because you're a construction company. They work for you and stay with you because of how you make them feel and how you invest in them to grow personally. That's the 'Why.' It's real, even if it isn't as tangible."

"I read that book after you recommended it to me," Chris said eagerly. "The example company he used in the book is Apple. People didn't connect with them because they were a computer company; they connected because they were convinced they would change the world."

"And they happened to use computers to do it," Alan agreed.

"You attract who you are," Amanda said emphatically. "Those are some of the intangibles that make up the 'Why.'"

"Precisely," Alan agreed. "That belief in the 'Why' attracted some of the top talent worldwide to come work for Apple."

"And created a diehard fan club," Daniel said, shaking his head. "I'm an Apple guy, I admit it!"

"Why else do you work here?" Alan repeated. "Are there other intangibles that are core drivers for you? What about your team? Let's take a few minutes and write some thoughts down."

Alan then led a discussion around the room based on the notes everyone took. After some debate and wordsmithing, the 'Why' finally emerged.

"What do you think?" Alan asked.

"Reynolds Industries exists to create a great work environment, striving to become the industry leader in workforce development," Amanda read off the whiteboard.

"I like it!" Chris exclaimed. "I think it's exactly why I keep showing up to work. I love seeing people become the best version of themselves."

"It's unusual for blue-collar trades," Scott said, "but I think it's exactly why I like being here."

"And if you like being here, Jake likes being here, Chris likes being here, Luke likes being here, and even Amanda likes being here..." Alan said teasingly, looking at Amanda, "Do you think other like-minded people would love to work here?"

"Well," Amanda said, leaning back. "What would the company look like if everyone had our core values and believed in why we are here?"

"I think – "

Daniel cut Alan off before he could answer, "Amazing, that's what it would look like—frickin' amazing!"

"Once you know 'Who' you are and 'Why' you're here, the 'What' and the 'How' are less relevant," Alan concurred. "Those are both important, don't get me wrong. But if you had a team that held these same core principles, you could be building skyscrapers, or you could all become professional dog walkers. The 'What' and 'How' should always be informed by the 'Who' and the 'Why.'"

"We still need competent people, though," Scott said, furrowing his brow. "We can't do the work we do if we had hired a bunch of dog walkers."

"Fair enough," Alan said. "That is the reason for the ADC in the Culture Check. Do they have the Ability? Let me ask you this: would you prefer to buy or develop talent instead?

"If we could get the most experienced people on our team, wouldn't that be good?" Scott replied.

"In my experience, you hire for attitude and then aptitude. If someone is humble and able to learn, developing that talent will pay dividends far more than simply hiring the 'most experienced' person. Many companies and sports teams make the mistake of throwing together top talent, packaging it to look good, and getting funding. It can work, but there are many egos in the world of 'talent.' It can often be way more of a headache than it is worth."

"But if people have our ethos and are willing to learn, the sky's the limit with how we can mentor, coach, and lead them."

"You got it, Scott," Alan concurred. "And that is exactly 'Why' you're here!"

Core Message

"Now that we have our 'Why,' it needs to inform our 'What' and our 'How,'" Alan continued. "'What' does Reynolds Industries do better than anyone else? 'How' do you do what you do that is unique?"

"That's pretty straightforward," Amanda began. "We are the leader in solving complex commercial construction problems."

"Is that accurate?" Alan challenged.

"It sure seems like it," Chris said with a nod. "In our region, anyway. Even our competitors call us when they have a tricky problem that we help walk them through."

"What else are you known for?" Alan asked.

"We are known for doing the right thing, even if it hurts in the short term," Ted stated.

"What do you mean by that?" Alan pressed.

"Last month, we had an issue with one of the projects that was delayed because the material didn't arrive on time. The owner was stressed because we were so close to wrapping up, and if we didn't meet the deadline, it would cost him a bunch. We had the right to delay it since the material delay wasn't our fault, but we got some guys to volunteer for overtime, and we got back on schedule. It was a little painful for a week, but the owner was blown away."

"So, you solve complex problems and sincerely care for your clients?"

"Yep, I think we are known for that. It's a reputation we have," Chris concurred.

"Why did this come so easily?" Amanda asked. "It took a lot longer for us to figure out our 'Why.'"

"I think it's similar to how 'Operations' come naturally when we create the Roles and Responsibilities Chart," Alan replied. "You're already doing 'the thing,' but now we are just articulating it for everyone else."

"The 'What' and 'How' you can put on a billboard, Amanda," Daniel said teasingly.

"I thought we already did!" she shot back with a grin.

"So, to put this all on the board," Alan continued, "Reynolds Industries is a MEP Contractor – 'What.' Known for solving complex building problems and taking fanatical care of their clients – 'How.' Because they are intent on creating a great work environment; striving to become the industry leader in workforce development – 'Why.'"

"I'd work there," Scott volunteered.

Grinning, Alan replied, "And do you think there are more people out there who would also want to come work here with this in mind?"

"I sure hope so!" he responded.

Grand Horizons

"Who, What, Where, When, Why, and How," Scott said.

"Huh?" Amanda responded, puzzled.

"Those are the question words," Scott explained. "It's something I remember from when I was a kid. My mom told me about them. I was trying to figure out what else we need for the vision."

"Good catch, Scott!" Alan said encouragingly. "We've tackled the 'Who,' 'What,' 'Why,' and 'How.' We need to determine the 'Where' and 'When.' 'When' is iterative; we never *fully* arrive, but we need milestones along the way with targets."

"Just like with the goal-setting work we did last time," Amanda interjected.

"Exactly," Alan confirmed. "We are still on track for the goals we set last time. Next month, when we dive into Strategy, we'll look more closely at setting near- and mid-term targets. We need to create a long-term vision for answering 'Where.' Where are we going? What does the horizon look like? What would the wildest version of success look like if we dream for a minute? I call this the 10-Year Horizon."

"Horizon, like looking through the cockpit on an airplane?" Chris inquired.

"Or like driving through Kansas. All you see is a horizon that never ends," Scott added.

"I was thinking more like a ship on the ocean," Alan said approvingly. "But both of those work as well. The idea is that we don't know exactly what we will encounter; these aren't necessarily goals, but they are general headings and directions for 'Where' we are going. This could be ten years out; this could be 50 years out. None of us have a crystal ball to predict the future, but we must be headed somewhere with purpose and intention. The author Jim Collins calls this the 'BHAG,' the Big Hairy Audacious Goal."

"You do steal some of your best ideas, Alan." Daniel joked.

"I can barely think a month out," Scott replied. "Let alone a year or 10!"

"That's why it takes a team to dream," Alan responded.

"That was super corny," Amanda said dryly. "But I get what you mean."

"Hopefully, you didn't steal that one," Daniel said with a smile. "It wasn't your best idea."

As everyone laughed at Daniel's quick wit, Alan replied, "If it sticks with you, then it was at least effective! Does everyone understand the exercise? When we look into the future, where do you see Reynold's Industries? What does it look like? Let's take 10 minutes to dream and jot down some ideas. Then we can compare, debate, and see what's on the horizon for us."

After gathering feedback from the team, identifying key elements, and debating what made the most sense, a 10-Year Horizon emerged.

"Ten years from now, Reynolds Industries will have offices in two other states outside Montana. We will be the leader in MEP innovation in the Western United States. We will have a world-class training program and be known as a 'magnet company' where the best of the best want to work. Most of our work will be sole-source contracts because of our reputation."

"You sure say 'we' a lot," Daniel teased. "Are you coming to work for us full-time yet?"

"Not exactly!" Alan smiled. "Even though I'm not here in the trenches full-time, I feel invested in helping everyone become their absolute best. So, if it's all right, I'll keep saying 'we'?"

"You're stuck with us now!" Chris exclaimed. "You are coming back next month, right?"

"Sure thing," Alan confirmed. "I'm excited to see how the Weekly Meeting goes between now and then. It also allows us to reflect on what we write down today and become more confident with the Vision. Next month, we dive into Strategy. In my opinion, this is where the magic happens!"

"Pretty sure we're all feeling some magic already," Scott replied. "I can't wait to see how it's all coming together."

Strategic Vision Page

Another month had passed since the last meeting with Alan, and the team at Reynolds Industries had started discussing their core values unofficially around the shop. This led to a renewed energy that Chris hadn't seen in years. As everyone gathered for the meeting, there was a palpable excitement about discussing strategy with Alan.

"Now that we're all settled in," Alan began, "let me introduce you to the Strategic Vision Page (SVP)."

"Sounds fancy," Amanda mused.

"It's one of those simple tools with a huge impact," Alan responded. "We started filling in some pieces last time. Let me show you where we're headed."

Alan handed everyone a double-sided sheet of paper.

"I'm going to like this!" Daniel exclaimed. "We'll all be on the same page—literally!"

"That's the goal," Alan replied. "Not just for you in this leadership team, but for everyone in the company. After today, we'll set a date for Reynolds Industries' first 'All Hands Meeting.'"

"We did the Core Values, Core Message, and 10-Year Horizon last time," Chris noted, "but why are those sections still blank?"

"That's because," Alan grinned, "this is your first pop quiz. Can everyone, from memory, write down the Core Values of Reynolds Industries?"

After several seconds of silence, Daniel said, "Hmm… maybe I'm not going to like this."

Alan smiled, "If the leadership team doesn't embody and remember the Core Values, you can't expect anyone else to buy in. We developed them just a month ago, and we're still testing how well they fit. So, let's take some time to review and start filling out the SVP."

After several minutes of discussion, the team filled out the first section of the SVP.

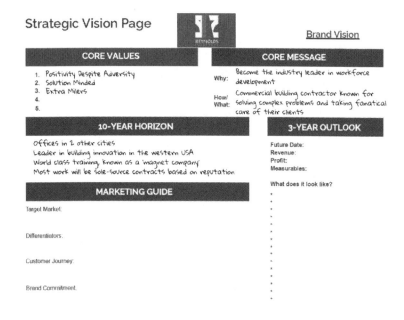

"Believe it or not," Alan began, "we'll have the rest of the SVP filled out by the end of the day. Let me explain the SVP a bit more. The first page is the Brand Vision —

answering big questions about Core Values, Core Message, 10-year Horizon, Marketing Guide, and 3-year Outlook. This mid- and long-term thinking will guide us as we build our strategy practically and tactically."

"Which is page two," Chris stated.

"Precisely," Alan replied. "The second page of the SVP covers the 1-Year Plan, Next 90, and Long-Term Issues that need addressing to achieve the 1-Year and 3-Year."

"Wait," Chris began to object, "this will show everyone how much revenue and profit we make. I don't think that's a good idea; some people already think I hoard cash. If they saw our annual revenue…"

As his voice trailed off, Amanda spoke up, "So what? I see the numbers every day, and I'm not breaking down your door for a raise. It's not like *you* made $3M last year; that's just the company's revenue."

"Yeah, but most guys don't know how that works," Chris protested.

"That's why you're going to teach them," Alan responded. "The more information the team has, the more transparent you are, the less guessing and rumors there will be. By teaching everyone the basics of business finance, they'll see how they contribute to the bottom line. Ideally, you tie incentives to growth and performance against profit goals."

"It would be nice to be rewarded for kicking butt," Scott chimed in.

"Exactly," Alan replied. "Show the team how their efforts impact the company's bottom line and tie that to incentives. You'll have a motivated, empowered workforce."

"How are we going to do that, though?" Chris asked. "It's not like we have great margins."

"Turnover," Amanda said flatly. "If we didn't have so much turnover, we'd have better margins."

"Happy teams make happy customers, which make happy, healthy companies," Alan stated. "Amanda, what would help reduce the turnover rate?"

"Well," Amanda began, "I think it's related to the Core Values we discussed."

"Dylan didn't make it," Scott interjected. "We had a Strike 1 conversation with him, and he quit and stormed out."

"And then what?" Alan probed.

"A couple of the guys thanked me," Chris said. "Everyone came together, and we're getting the same work done with less attitude. Kyle's attitude has changed a lot. We also had the Strike 1 conversation with him, but he seems to understand our aim to create a better work environment."

"He's been easier to work with," Scott agreed. "Amanda might be right — the Core Values are key."

"Wasn't my idea!" Amanda protested. "This was Alan's brainchild!"

"He probably stole that good idea, though," Daniel said with a wink.

"I can't take credit for the idea of Core Values," Alan laughed. "I won't take credit for having a vision or creating goals. None of these principles are a brand-new idea."

"Then why do so many businesses struggle?" Chris asked.

"For the same reason, most people aren't healthy," Alan responded. "It's no secret that you need to eat right and exercise to stay healthy. Most people aren't healthy because they don't have a plan, a guide, or both."

"That's what the Strategic Vision Page does," Scott mused. "I think I'm back to liking it again." Daniel interrupted. "And I still like you, Alan, even after you fired us all!"

After the laughter died down, Chris raised his hand. "I still have my question, though; I agree that Core Values and the Culture Check are game changers. And it makes sense that if we taught everyone some finance basics, they could see how running a company works. But how do we keep people and avoid them getting poached? If they had that information and went to work for a competitor, wouldn't that hurt us? I'm happy to tie incentives to company growth, rewarding effective and profitable work... But where do we even start?"

"We don't have to create the incentive plan today," Alan responded. "Let's just set revenue and profit targets by writing them down. Before we get there, though, let's tackle the most important part of building a strategy—the Marketing Guide."

Marketing Guide

Alan continued by asking a simple question: "What do you think of when I say 'Marketing'?"

"Flyers, trade shows, radio commercials, social media, email…" Amanda started listing off. "I get junk all the time for so many things."

"Advertising is part of marketing, but it's not everything," Alan responded. "Marketing is about how you position yourself in the marketplace. It speaks to your vision, differentiators, secret sauce, ideal customers, and how you do what you do. When people think of marketing, they typically think of lead generation. I will challenge you to consider' internal' and 'external' marketing. When you have alignment with Core Values and a vision that people can rally around, you must ensure your team understands that vision. This means communication and marketing."

"Ah, the old 5 W's and the H again," Scott mused.

"You're good at this," Daniel teased. "I think you should be running this meeting, Scott!"

"Whoa, now," Scott smiled defensively. "I just know the question words, that's all."

"Let's go through the question words," Alan encouraged. "Who, What, and Where helps define your target audience.

Who are they? – demographic: What do they care about? – psychographic: Where do they live? – geographic."

"Psychographic..." Daniel said intently. "Yep, that's a big word I didn't know. Alan, you're still hired."

"Not taking over the meeting either, Daniel?" Scott joked back.

"The questions are the important part," Alan assured. "So, let's tackle them. When talking about your ideal customer, who are they, what do they care about, and where do they live?"

"We do a lot of work with commercial builders, but we also work with individual owners on custom projects," Chris said.

"That's fine," Alan assured. "We will need to answer these questions for both market segments. Let's start with commercial builders. That's the 'who' question. Where do they live, and what do they care about?"

"We only build in certain markets," Amanda responded. "But the companies are all over the place throughout the Northwest US."

"And what do they care about?" Alan asked.

"They care about communication," Chris said. "They know that construction schedules can get off track for various reasons but want over-the-top communication about it."

"And do you communicate over the top with them?" Alan inquired.

"Absolutely," Chris said confidently. "That's part of our reputation and why they like working with us."

"That sounds like the beginning of the marketing 'why' as well," Alan responded. "Who – commercial contractors; Where – Northwest United States; What – constant communication. Now we need to answer the question 'Why.'"

"I see what you did there!" Daniel said. "These are all pieces of the Marketing Guide section of the SVP. Target Market is Who, What, and Where. Differentiators are Why, Process is How, and Promise is When."

"Now I'm getting lost," Scott stated. "Can we go back to the first part?"

"Sure, let's review," Alan answered, returning to the whiteboard. "I'll put it up on the board so we can see where we are."

Alan wrote on the board as he spoke: "Who – commercial builders; Where – Northwest US; What – communication."

"We have the first target market, so let's talk Differentiators," Alan resumed. "Why do people choose you over your competitors? What are your Differentiators? What makes Reynolds Industries unique?"

"Over-communication is one Differentiator," Chris responded. "And we solve complex problems that others can't, which is probably another one."

"And we're great at creating timelines and deadlines," Scott interjected. "No construction project is perfect, but we try not to overpromise. We've all seen people overpromise on timelines and then fall behind, messing up everyone's schedule."

"We've lost jobs because our timelines were 'too slow' though," Amanda noted.

"But then what happens?" Chris asked rhetorically. "The builder comes to us in the future because our timeline was more accurate."

"And we over-communicate and solve complex problems," Scott said.

"I think we have our Differentiators," Alan responded. "Now, we need to determine How and When. How do you work with clients on their customer journey? And when they work with you, what is your guarantee or promise to them?"

"I see what you're saying now, Daniel," Scott exclaimed. "Another reason you don't want me leading this meeting. Alan, you're still hired!"

"Good to hear!" Alan responded. "Let's tackle the Customer Journey and 'How' you work with clients. What process do you use that gives clients confidence that you know what you're doing? Let's pretend I'm a new contractor with a project, and I've never heard of Reynolds Industries before. What is the process from start to finish?"

After discussing the complexities of the MEP components of the construction process, Alan guided the team through simplifying it. What emerged was a customer journey that looked more like an infographic than a lengthy list of bullet points.

"And when I hire you as the subcontractor, what promise do you make about your work?"

"What do you mean promise?" Amanda asked. "We either did the work correctly, or we didn't."

"If you stand by your work, you want to spell out if there are any warranty or guarantee," Alan responded.

"Our warranty is twice as long as the industry standard," Chris explained. "We are required to warranty our work per state law. The equipment we install has manufacturing warranties, but doesn't everyone already know that?"

"I didn't know that until you just told me." Alan explained, "I would venture to guess that people outside the construction world don't know that either. It doesn't hurt to spell that out; it builds confidence."

"I talk about it with new builders we haven't worked with before." Daniel said, "But I love the idea of spelling it out clearly, especially for residential clients."

"We want to end up with a one-pager that defines whom we work with best, what they care about, the process of working with us, and how we stand by our work." Alan explained, "I can send you some examples, and I would encourage you to create that one-pager by the next Quarterly meeting."

"I can do that," Daniel stated, "Can you please create a To-Do for me, Amanda?"

"Marketing Guide complete," Alan said emphatically. "Going back to our earlier discussion about culture fit, the Core Values inform everyone in your company about the people you're looking for. The Marketing Guide helps your employees understand what an ideal client looks like, what they expect, how they want to be treated, and the process of how they work with your company. This is the 'internal' marketing piece of the SVP that informs the one-pager and all 'external' marketing to your clients."

"Attracting the right kind of people needs to be a core values fit and also understand the type of clients we work with," Chris said thoughtfully. "That makes a lot of sense. If someone is a core value fit but only wants to work on spec homes, we may not be the place for them."

"And it clarifies how we work with clients from start to finish," Scott added. "I think this will be super helpful for our current team."

"That's the goal," Alan responded. "A few more sections and the SVP will be ready for its debut to the rest of the company."

3-Year Outlook

"Now we need to bring this from a 30,000-foot view down to a 10,000-foot view," Alan stated. "Having a solid grasp of the Core Vision and Marketing Guide, we are now going to figure out the 3-Year Outlook."

"This is where we do some actual projections?" Amanda asked.

"Correct." Alan responded, "Based on what we have done in the past few years and the year-over-year growth that has happened, if we project that into the future, where do we end up?"

"This is the part that I wasn't too excited about." Chris mused.

"This is the part that I'm excited about!" Scott replied, "I have only had a general idea of what we've done, but since I haven't seen the company's financials, I have no idea where we are."

"Time to dive into it then." Alan said enthusiastically, "If it helps, Chris, the 3-Year Outlook isn't *just* about financials; it is also about casting a vision of what the near future looks like. The point of growing the company isn't so that you just have more money. Money is the tool that allows you to do the things that you want to do as a team."

"What do we want it to look like then?" Amanda asked.

"That question, Amanda," Alan responded, "Is an excellent place to start! Take five to ten minutes and write down what you envision the company looking like three years from now, based on the 10-Year Horizon. Don't be afraid to get more specific. How many people work here? What types of jobs will you be doing? Where will you be geographically? What do you think the revenue will be?"

After everyone spent some time writing down their thoughts, Alan continued. "Now, let's talk through the revenue and profit numbers. We have varying numbers, so let's get some consensus on what kind of growth we will see over the next few years."

"I don't see us doing more than $9 Million," Chris stated intently.

"Come on, Chris," Daniel countered, "We just bid a job last week that was close to $1 Million alone; you don't think there will be more and bigger jobs that we will be asked to do?"

"Especially as we get better organized, communication increases, and the team's morale improves?" Scott concurred.

"Let's look back at the 10-Year Horizon." Alan added, "If you want to be the leader in the Western United States and have another office outside of this area, it's going to require us to stretch a bit."

"We have the team to do it." Ted stated, "I think we will be closer to $12 Million in the next three years at the rate we have been growing."

"Outside of any huge financial collapse," Amanda continued, "I think we are going to grow quite a bit; maybe not $12 Million, but more than $10 Million."

"So, $11 Million?" Alan asked.

"Even that is a stretch." Chris reiterated, "I'm all for growth, and I hear what you are all saying. But that is some serious growth from where we are right now; it's more than double!"

"What did we do last year again?" Scott inquired.

"$4.7 million, " Amanda replied, "And I think we are on track for around $6.5 million this year."

"But what if we don't hit it?" Chris asked. "I hate setting a goal I can't achieve."

"Think of it less of a goal that you *have* to hit and more of an outlook of where you are headed." Alan reassured him, "That's why I call it the 3-Year Outlook. We may be above or below the number; we may or may not have the number of employees we project, the various locations, etc. What it does, though, is give us a more tangible picture of where we are headed. One that is realistically within our grasp."

"All right then," Chris said. "If you all have my back, let's say $11 million in the next three years."

"LET'S GO!!!" Daniel shouted. " I'm sorry. I'm just getting kind of excited about this stuff."

"I appreciate the enthusiasm, Daniel." Alan replied. "Let's keep working through this 3-Year Outlook. What do we project our profit to be?"

"What do you mean by profit, exactly?" Amanda asked, "Like Gross Margin, Net Profit, or EBITDA?"

"I'm not even sure what all of those mean," Scott interjected.

"Good time for a quick financial lesson, then." Alan said, "Gross margin is all revenue minus COGS or cost of goods sold. As a percentage, you would take the gross margin divided by your revenue."

"Looking at last year, for example, we did $4.7 Million in revenue, and our COGS were $3.23 Million." Amanda replied, "That means our gross margin percentage was 31.3%."

"What are the other ones then?" Scott asked.

"Our Net Profit was $293,000, meaning our net profit percentage was 6.2%," Amanda replied.

"Which is a little low for your industry." Alan responded, "And when you see how the expenses break down and show it to your team, they realize that Chris isn't hoarding cash; it is being used to keep the company moving forward. Paying for wages, equipment, benefits, etc."

"Then what was that itty-bitty-ya thing?" Scott inquired.

"EBITDA," Amanda replied, "Earnings before interest, taxes, depreciation, and amortization."

"Yep, not sure what any of the words mean except for taxes!" Scott said with a chuckle.

Alan laughed as well, "It's just another way to look at the company's operational financial health. For now, I recommend we keep it simple. Whatever we use, it needs to stay consistent."

"Let's just make it net profit, then." Chris stated, "And I would like to be in a healthier place in 3 years so that we can do the things we want to do, like build a bigger shop."

"What do we want to target then, Chris?" Alan inquired.

"If we can fix the turnover rate, I bet we can get over 10%," Amanda said.

"What about 11 – 11?" Scott asked, "$11 Million, 11% Profit. Makes it easy to remember."

"As long as it's a target and not a goal," Chris responded, "I'm in."

"Great," Alan continued, "let's talk about measurables then. The Measurable should be something your team can get excited about seeing continue to go up."

"Like the billions served at McDonalds?" Daniel asked, "Remember when that was a big thing years ago?"

"Exactly like that." Alan concurred, "I'm not sure what it would be for this industry. Maybe it's the number of square feet built or the number of five-star reviews. The idea is that it is continually growing and a measuring stick to look back on."

"I like the idea of the number of square feet built." Scott said, "It ties directly to what we do all day, every day."

"Works for me." Chris agreed, "It will be fun figuring that out going back since we started."

After some discussion, refining, and combining, the 3-Year Outlook came to life with revenue, profit, and measurables. A handful of bullet points also emerged, which painted a picture of what the near future held for the team.

"Last thing before we take a break," Alan said, "Close your eyes for a minute and imagine Reynolds Industries three years from now. In three years, Reynolds Industries will have made $11 Million in revenue with an 11% net profit margin and will have completed over 500,000 square feet of building in its lifetime. We will have around 30 RPRS employees on the team. A new engineering division alongside the actual building will be launched. We will have moved into a new shop to handle the company's growth. 20% of the jobs come as sole source contracts. And there will be the first 'class' of new hires who have completed the new world-class training program…"

"LET'S GO!!" Daniel shouted again.

The SVP was now really beginning to take shape.

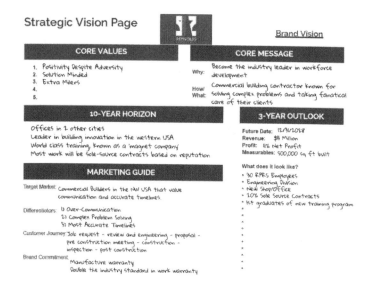

The Back Page

"Let's dive into the back page." Alan continued, "Here, we are going to spell out the 1-Year Plan and what we need to do in the Next 90 days to keep us on track towards that 1-Year Plan. We want to be more specific on the 1-Year Plan because these are the goals we will do everything we can to accomplish. Now, we move from the 10,000-foot view to the 5,000-foot view."

"Putting revenue and profit numbers should be easier." Amanda thought out loud.

"Easy for *you*." Scott teased.

"I had already figured it out, remember?" Amanda reminded him, "We are on track for $6.5 Million this year."

"What profit margin, though?" Chris asked.

"Not great, it's a bit down from last year so far."

"What could we do to make it better?" Alan pressed.

"I think we are doing it." Amanda responded, "As we discussed earlier, if we create a high-functioning team and decrease our turnover, I think the profit margin should go back up."

"What is the best-case scenario for the profit margin you see for this year, Amanda?" Chris inquired.

"I think we could hit 8%." Amanda replied, "From what I've seen so far on the team, how attitudes have improved, and we are tracking numbers weekly; I think we could do 8% if we stay diligent."

"Works for me," Chris stated. "More margin, the better."

"How likely are you to hit that target?" Alan probed, "I ask because the 1-Year Plan needs to be more definite. We don't need to make goals that are a 100% slam dunk because that doesn't push us. On the other hand, we don't want to make goals so out of the realm of possibility that people don't buy into them. Ideally, you have a goal that is around 70%-80% possible. This gets the buy-in from the team you need. They see it's possible, and at the same time, they know it isn't just going to happen. Everyone is an integral part of making the goal a reality."

"In that case, we should move the target to $7 Million." Daniel added, "If we are already on track for $6.5 Million, then the extra $500k should be what stretches us."

"Those both check out for me." Chris said, "Based on where we are so far this year, if we hone things and push a bit more, $7 million and an 8% profit margin are within that possible range."

"Let's write it on the SVP then!" Alan said encouragingly, "And how many square feet were built for our measurable?"

"We should be close to 200,000 square feet," Scott replied.

"To be more specific," Amanda added, "I calculated the measurable to be 185,000 square feet built."

"That sounds perfect," Alan said approvingly. "With that in mind, do you remember the Eisenhower Matrix from our first meeting? Based on the 3-Year Outlook, what must we accomplish this year to ensure we are on track? What are the things that are important but not necessarily urgent? Let's take about ten minutes and write some thoughts down."

After everyone had finished writing down their thoughts, Alan brought the focus back to the conversation. Going around the room, people gave their lists to Alan, who wrote everything down on the whiteboard. Through a process of combination and elimination, the final list emerged that became the goals for the 1-Year Plan.

"Now that we have the 1-Year Plan, what does the Next 90 Days look like?" Alan asked.

"Same idea?" Scott inquired. "Based on what we need to have accomplished with the 1-Year Plan, what is most important for the Next 90 Days?"

"Exactly." Alan confirmed, "And if you recall from our first meeting together when we set the first 90-day goals. These goals will require milestones to stay on track toward the bigger objective."

"This makes complete sense to me." Amanda said, "I think I naturally do this anyway. I call it back planning."

"That's a great way to put it," Alan said, returning to draw on the whiteboard. "If I return to my altitude analogies, it will look like this. I call it Goal Planning to the Now. Based on the Core Values and Core Message, where do we want to be in 10 Years? Based on the 10-Year Horizon, where do we want to be in 3-Years? Based on the 3-Year Outlook, what must we do this year? Based on the 1-Year Plan, what must we accomplish in the Next 90 days? Based on the goals for the next 90 days, what milestones must be achieved and when? Based on these milestones, what do I need to do this week? Based on what I need to do this week, what do I need to do today? This helps set your priorities daily. It is all designed to create purposeful motion toward the greater objective."

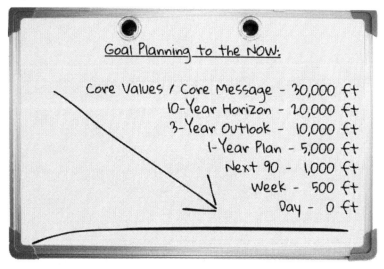

"And when everyone has thought through the steps and turned the tasks into milestones, we have visibility into where each other are in relation to the goals," Chris stated.

"And accountability," Ted interjected.

"That is why for the 1-Year Plan and Next 90, we talked about the most important things we need to accomplish. Because if we, as the leadership team, determine that these are the most important things, then we should welcome accountability. We all know that doing our part is vital to the success of the whole."

"What about the Long-Term Issues list?" Chris asked, "Aren't we handling issues as they come up in the Weekly Meetings?"

"Great question." Alan replied, "Today, we are tackling some Long-Term Issues because it is part of the greater Meeting Cadence. Most issues will be handled at the Weekly Meetings, resulting in a short-term To-Do as the next step. Other issues you will find won't be resolved in a week or two and will likely need attention for a quarterly objective like what we set today. Those issues need a place to live that isn't on the Weekly Meeting."

Striding back to the whiteboard, Alan drew and labeled three distinct compartments.

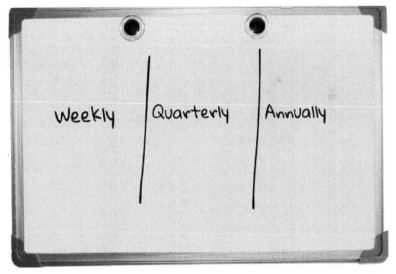

"Most issues are resolved at the Weekly Meeting. Larger issues that require more time and coordination become quarterly issues that we solve through creating the Next 90 Goals. Finally, the bigger vision questions like Core Values, Marketing, 10-Year, and 3-Year are discussed and revised during the Annual Planning Meeting, along with the 1-Year Plan."

"So, we are going to see you next quarter?" Scott asked.

"That's the plan." came Alan's reply, "The back page of the SVP is refreshed every quarter with the Next 90, and the entire SVP is refreshed every year as we continue to dream and adapt to the market and environment we find ourselves in at the time. That's a two-day meeting to refresh and celebrate wins from the previous year, realign as a team, and reevaluate the SVP."

"But our Core Values shouldn't change, though," Amanda said, concerned.

"They rarely change, but you may find that they need to be refreshed or another one added as you find something missing." Alan replied, "The next step after today, though, is to present the SVP to the team at an 'All Hands Meeting.' I'll send you some ideas about the best way to present and get buy-in from everyone. As you present the annual and quarterly objectives, this 'All Hands Meeting' will become a regular part of the company's meeting cadence every quarter. You also recap how the team did in the previous quarter."

"I think the guys are going to appreciate this." Scott mused, "I just wish they could have been in the process of putting it together. I think some of them would have a different attitude about it."

"Hold on," Amanda interrupted, "going back to the refresh of the SVP every year; our Core Values shouldn't change, though, right?"

"You may find that they need to be refreshed or another one added as you find something missing." Alan replied, "I find that this is the perfect balance for those that are highly structured and those that are highly flexible. Finding the balance and framework to work from is what is important."

"The Framework." Chris stated emphatically, "That's what we should call it, The Framework. It's structured enough that we stay on track but gives us the freedom to adapt as we need to."

"I think I'm going to steal that idea, Chris." Alan said, smiling, "I usually steal my best ideas."

Epilogue

"How was your time in Europe?" Alan asked excitedly.

"Unbelievable." Came Chris's response. "If you had told me five years ago that I would have been able to take six weeks away from the company to go on a vacation with my family out of the country, I would have thought you were out of your mind!"

"What have you found now that you've been back this last week?"

"Honestly," Chris continued in a hushed tone, "I think the team did better without me here. I've found a few things that Scott needed some coaching on. Mostly around timelines and communication with some of the new foremen. Besides that, I was amazed to see how well everything ran without me."

"I'm sure you will uncover more inefficiencies and places where the team can use your insight. You do an excellent job of pushing people in a way that they respond to." Alan encouraged, "I wouldn't take yourself out of the company completely yet!"

"Ha!" Chris chuckled, "Not planning on doing that, but rolling out the Employee Stock Ownership Plan earlier this year was huge!"

"Tell me more." Alan probed encouragingly.

"When we had those first few meetings as you introduced us to The Framework, I couldn't see how showing the finances to the team would be helpful."

"And now?"

"Now, I wouldn't think of doing it any other way."

"I don't think there is a 'one-size-fits-all' approach to anything in life," Alan responded, "but I'm so glad to hear that it is working for you and the team!"

"We recently won an award as well." Chris continued.

"Another one? What was this one for?"

"This one came from an industry association, we were voted 'Best MEP Contractor in the United States!'"

"Sounds like you're five years ahead of your original 10-Year Horizon!" Alan said excitedly, "Congrats, Chris, it is a testament to who you have become as a leader. The leadership development program you created is inspiring."

"I think you're the true hero in all of this," Chris responded.

"Not at all," Alan replied, "You, as the founder, taking the risk, creating an incredible company for people to be a part of, changing the communities and lives of people in those communities; *that's* heroic. I'm just glad that I could guide you in the right direction."

"Mentor, Coach, Lead, right?" Chris quipped, "Thanks for everything, coach... happy birthday!"

Part Two:
The Framework

Overview

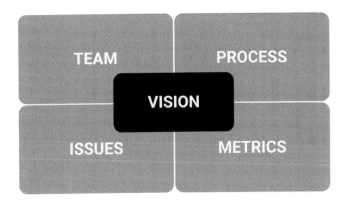

The goal of authoring this book this way was to share what you need to do and how to implement and use The Framework in your business.

The Framework is a systematic way to run your company. The five main focal points are the business's fundamentals (Vision, Team, Process, Metrics, and Issues). If you've read the book and, at some point, thought, "This isn't rocket science," you're right.

If you already have a way to run your company and a systematic approach to keeping things structured, keep doing what you're doing if it works.

If it isn't working, I challenge you to implement The Framework for your company. Some of the benefits we have seen from companies that use The Framework are:

Quantitative

- Increased Retention Rate
- Increased Productivity
- Increased Customer Satisfaction
- Measurable, Sustainable Growth
- Increased Profitability

Qualitative

- Happy, cohesive team
- Clear, unified vision
- Work *ON* the business, not just *IN* the business
- Quality of Life for the owners and employees

I can appreciate those who want to do it themselves. If that is you, let this guide be your reference as you do your team meetings, formulate a vision, and create the business you've always wanted.

I suggest a 90-day rollout, where you meet with your team for a full day offsite once a month for three months, just like Alan did with Reynolds Industries. At the end of the third month, you do a company-wide rollout 'All Hands Meeting' (see the Tool Kit Section).

If you want help implementing The Framework, we would be glad to see if a Framework Coach would fit your situation well. Please send an email to info@leadcademy.com.

Vision

"Where there is no vision, the people perish…"

The beginning of every enterprise, artistic endeavor, or journey requires a vision. The vision can be as simple as wanting to be in control of your own life or as complex as a multi-national corporation. It can be as simple as going to the park or as complex as climbing Mount Everest.

Having a vision in your mind is one thing; seeing it realized in the world is another. Bringing on a team that shares that vision is even more vital.

Many companies I've worked with didn't start with a grand vision. Most of the time, it was something straightforward. Over time, as the company grows, there needs to be a constant reminder about the vision and where you're headed as a company. There are plenty of places for people to work, but is there a larger, more inspiring future vision that you can see?

This is equally important in people's personal lives. During the Annual Planning Session, I encourage companies to reflect, write down, and share personal goals in these four areas: Financial, Educational, Spiritual, and Relational.

When we help people on our team develop a vision for their life *outside* of work, it also helps align them *at* work to see how their personal vision and the company vision coincide.

Components of the Vision, outlined in the Strategic Vision Page (SVP) are:

- Core Values – Who are you as a company?
- Core Message – Why are you in business?
- 10-Year Horizon – Where are you headed?
- 3-Year Outlook – What does it look like?
- Marketing Guide – How do you do what you do?

Answering these fundamental questions gives the team guidance and direction on how to make decisions. If there is a grey area, understanding the 'Why' based on 'Who we are' becomes the north star to help inform these decisions.

Book Resources:

- *Start with Why* – Simon Sinek
- *Visioneering* – Andy Stanley

Team

I've been on many teams over my lifetime. I played sports teams while growing up and still play recreational soccer. Music teams when playing in different bands. Volunteer teams when I worked with churches and non-profits. Business teams across various companies.

Much has been written and spoken about when it comes to creating a compelling team. Within The Framework, I wanted to distill the concepts down into three tools that I believe can help shape your team:

1) **Culture Check** – Not everyone in the world fits every organization. When I first introduced The Framework to their company, I told people I may not fit them because of my core values. I have a high regard for people and think they are the greatest asset to your team. The fact that they have been entrusted to you to lead is not something to take lightly. I'm not a good fit if a team cares about winning at all costs, regardless of who they hurt. Once core values are defined, this becomes the standard to see if a person or potential hire is a culture fit. If they aren't a culture fit, don't worry... there are plenty of other people out there who are!

2) **Delegation Matrix** – Just like not every person is a fit for every team, not every person on your team is a fit

for every job on the team. It is hard for people who hate numbers to understand accountants and people who love numbers. A simple tool to help organizations as they grow is to have everyone fill out the Delegation Matrix to see what things they should be doing more of, less of, and what can be taken off their plate through delegation to someone who is better suited to the role. Which brings me to...

3) **Roles & Responsibilities Chart** – When I first worked with teams, I was amazed to see how often people accidentally stepped on each other's toes, doing the exact or similar functions. Clearly defining the R&R Chart delineates who is responsible for what. Once you have outlined the structure with roles and responsibilities, the organization will grow as you hire into the needed areas based on what you find in the Delegation Matrix.

Book Resources:

- *Extreme Ownership* – Jocko Willink
- *The Five Dysfunctions of a Team* – Patrick Lencioni

Process

In your business, there is a 'way' that you do things. When there are just one or two people on the team, it's easy to know how to do it. As the team grows, you will have to move away from 'tribal knowledge' and more towards creating the processes and procedures that can be trained and followed by new people in the organization.

McDonald's isn't known for having world-class burgers; it's known for selling the most burgers in the world. They have done that through systems and processes that anyone can follow.

Standardizing and documenting your processes make your company scalable. If only one person in the entire organization knows how to bid on a job, for example, that will become a bottleneck for your organization as no one else will know how to do it. Worse yet, everyone does it their way, creating mess, confusion, and headaches for everyone else.

I tell people to use the 80/20 Rule (the Pareto Principle since it was named after an Italian guy whose last name was...). The 80/20 rule when creating a process is to write down the main bullet points (the 20%) that will give you the intent and objective of the process (the 80%). This way, it defines the process that is documented but is not too overwhelming or burdensome. This will vary from industry to industry and job to job. The goal of creating the process is not to write down every minute step (unless you are manufacturing airplanes, then, in that case, follow EVERY step... please).

Once the process has been documented, it needs to be put somewhere that it is readily accessible to the person responsible for completing that task or process. For some companies, this means having a digital repository to which everyone has access. For others, it could be as simple as printing off paper and putting it in binders.

Whatever the distribution method, the important thing is that you are creating processes to hold people accountable. If people don't know what to do or how they should be doing it, trying to hold them accountable for something that only exists in their minds is not reasonable.

Book Resources:

* *Systemology* – David Jenyns

Metrics

I will never forget being in the meeting when someone asked, "So, what are your KPIs for this project?" I quickly grabbed my phone and searched 'What is a KPI?' – The response didn't help. 'A KPI is a Key Performance Indicator.' Thanks, Google, but what does it *mean!?*

I know I'm not the only one. When I ask business owners about metrics or KPIs for their company, the most common response is, "My bank account balance was higher at the end of the year than at the beginning, so we must be doing all right."

In a nutshell, metrics provide valuable insights into the health and performance of your company. It's the scoreboard telling you whether you're winning in different areas of your business.

Metrics are the indicators that tell you ahead of time if you are on track or off track with the business. Depending on seasonality, these numbers can change. The important thing is that you are tracking them.

There are several types of metrics that measure financial health, sales and marketing, growth, and operational efficiency. Understanding your numbers paints a clear picture of how you are doing and allows you to begin forecasting where you are going effectively. They also help you understand trends and seasonality. Lastly, they can provide benchmarks that you can use for training and in holding your teams accountable.

For those who like numbers and data, I always give one word of caution: *Metrics are indicators, not dictators.* Let the numbers help paint the picture, but don't make decisions from the numbers alone.

Book Resources:

- *Measure What Matters* – John Doerr

Issues

I love telling people that I have issues. I'm not alone, however. I have issues. You have issues. We all have issues. I have heard people say you don't let others see your weakness. That could be good advice if you're going into hand-to-hand combat, but not if you're running a company.

The issue with *not* bringing up issues is that everyone already knows your issues. Your team understands the issues you are facing. They need to know that *you* know that you have issues.

Bringing issues to the forefront of the conversation allows you, as the leader, to steer the discussion in the direction it needs to go. If you ignore issues or don't talk about them, people can come to wild conclusions about where the issue will take you.

In my experience, issues come from one of two places. They are either Team Issues or Process Issues.

If it is a Team Issue, refer to the Culture Check. If they are a culture fit but aren't doing a decent job in their role, the question is, do they have the Ability, Desire, and Capacity to fulfill the role?

If that all checks out, you have a Process Issue. Do you have a process? If not, you need one! If you do have a process, is there anything that needs to be modified in the process that will result in a better outcome? Did the person on the team doing the work not follow the process? That goes back to a Team Issue where you can talk with that person on your team and hold them accountable to the process, retrain, etc.

Some issues show a bigger systemic problem that may need to be handled with a quarterly or annual goal. Most issues that come up within the week will generally be resolved within the week.

Book Resources:

- *Radical Candor* – Kim Scott

Part Three:
The Tool Kit

Tool Kit Explainer

Throughout the book, I reference different tools that Alan uses to help the team implement various aspects of The Framework. I include them in this format for reference.

To download the entire Tool Kit Resource, please visit:

https://www.theframeworkbook.com/tool-kit

Here are some of the tools in the Tool Kit:

- ✓ Strategic Vision Page (SVP) w/ instructional guide
- ✓ The Framework Rollout Plan
- ✓ Scoreboard
- ✓ Weekly Meeting Agenda w/ instructional guide
- ✓ 1:1 Meeting Agenda w/ instructional guide
- ✓ SMART Goals Template
- ✓ Delegation Matrix
- ✓ Roles and Responsibilities Chart
- ✓ Culture Check
- ✓ 4 Strike Guide (Performance Improvement Plan)
- ✓ Quarterly Performance Review Template

Yes, you will be asked for your email to receive the Tool Kit. Think of it as an ethical bribe. I'll also periodically send over some information that you might find helpful on your business journey. Like any email list, if you don't find it helpful, feel free to unsubscribe – fair?

For more book recommendations, check out our book list:

www.leadcademy.com/book-list

Strategic Vision Page (SVP)

Strategic Vision Page

Brand Vision

CORE VALUES

1.
2.
3.
4.
5.

CORE MESSAGE

Why:

How/
What:

10-YEAR HORIZON

3-YEAR OUTLOOK

Future Date:
Revenue:
Profit:
Measurables:

What does it look like?

* * * * * * * * * * * * * * *

MARKETING GUIDE

Target Market:

Differentiators:

Customer Journey:

Brand Commitment:

Strategic Vision Page

1-YEAR PLAN

Future Date:
Revenue:
Profit:
Measurables:

Annual Goals:

NEXT 90

Future Date:
Revenue:
Profit:
Measurables:

Quarterly Goals:

LONG-TERM ISSUES

The Framework Rollout Plan

The purpose of implementing The Framework with the entire organization is so that everyone on the team is on the same page. The goal is to create camaraderie and teamwork for the company.

❏ Schedule a Date/Time for the entire company to get together for an 'All Hands Meeting.' These meetings typically take 1-2 hours.

❏ Have the Strategic Vision Page filled out entirely and approved by the leadership team before presenting it to everyone

❏ Have the Roles and Responsibilities Chart filled out and approved by the leadership team before presenting to everyone

❏ Have the Core Values Speech presented to the leadership team to sign off on before the meeting

❏ The Core Values Speech can be short and to the point, but best practice is to have each contain three elements:

  ❏ State the Core Value

  ❏ Bullet points of what the Core Value means

  ❏ Story of team member exemplifying the Core Value

❏ Have the three elements for each Core Value to help make them as straightforward as possible.

EXAMPLE:

"Help People First"

This means we maintain the relationship and are an excellent factor in every conversation. We help people, making their problem our problem as their ally so that we can fix issues together. An example was that Anthony was on the phone with a customer troubleshooting and realized that their phone handset was the issue as it was ancient. The person realizing this was upset because they were on a fixed income and were not sure when they would be able to get a new handset. Anthony let the customer know that we would send her one and then went online and purchased the phone himself, never asking for reimbursement or kudos, just because he wanted to help the customer. That's what we mean by 'Help People First.'

AGENDA:

❏ Explain the company's history so far and why there is a need for a better organization.

  ❏ Go through the Strategic Vision Page

  ❏ Core Values Speech

  ❏ Core Message: Why/What/How

  ❏ Marketing Guide

  ❏ Target Market

  ❏ Differentiators

  ❏ Customer Journey

  ❏ Brand Commitment

- ❏ 10-Year Horizon: Where we are headed

- ❏ 3 Year Goals

- ❏ 1 Year Plan

- ❏ This Quarter Goals/Objectives

BEST PRACTICES:

- ❏ Days/weeks before the meeting, leadership team members talk casually/informally to their teams about looking forward to it and how it will help. Set a positive example and tone ahead of time before the meeting.

- ❏ Owner/CEO of the company to present the history and needs of the company as well as present the Core Values Speech

- ❏ Other elements of the rollout can be presented by others on the leadership team, which helps create a united front.

- ❏ As others on the leadership team present, they can also highlight examples of the core values in action on their team.

- ❏ Leave some time for questions and feedback from the team

- ❏ Stay on track but try to avoid rushing out after the meeting; allow the time for team members to hang out and have a conversation instead of running straight back to work.

Scoreboard

RESPONSIBLE	METRIC	GOAL	3-Jan	10-Jan	17-Jan	24-Jan	31-Jan	7-Feb	14-Feb	21-Feb	28-Feb	7-Mar	14-Mar	21-Mar	28-Mar

COMPANY SCOREBOARD

Weekly Meeting Agenda

Date: _____

Time: _____

90 Minute Agenda:

Check-In   5 Minutes
(Personal/Professional)

Goals   5 Minutes
(On/Off Track)

Metrics   5 Minutes
(On/Off Track)

Headlines   5 Minutes
(Customers/Employees)

To-Dos   5 Minutes
(Done/Not Done)

Issues   60 Minutes
(Prioritize Top 3)

Wrap-Up   5 Minutes

Agenda Item Explanation:

➢ **Good News -** Check in with the team to build relationships and transition from working 'in' the business to working 'on' the business.

➢ **Goals** - Based on the milestones set, are your Goals currently on or off track? Any goal that is off track moves to the Issues List.

➢ **Metrics** - Key metrics that you are looking at every week that can show immediately if things are on or off track. Any metric that is off track moves to the Issues List.

➢ **Headlines -** Bring up information more like an announcement. If any headlines need more in-depth discussion, move to the Issues List.

➢ **To-Dos -** The action items from last week that were supposed to be finished within a week or two are reviewed and were either Done or Not Done. Whoever has the To-Do, whether Done or Not Done, can ask to move it to the Issues List.

➢ **Issues -** This is the core of the meeting, where the most important things that need to be discussed are.

➢ **Wrap-Up -** Recap the To-Dos to ensure everyone knows what they are doing this week. See if any messages must be shared with everyone at the Company Meeting. Rate the meeting. Anyone who rates the meeting lower than average must also give feedback on what could be better for next week.

Issues List best practice:

- ➢ Read through all the Issues.
- ➢ Decide whether to Keep, Kill, or Combine an Issue.
  - ○ *Keep* means it is still relevant and needs to be discussed.
  - ○ *Kill* means that it is no longer an issue.
  - ○ *Combine* means that it is a duplicate issue.
- ➢ Decide the top 3 issues that need to be discussed.
- ➢ Start with Issue 1 and don't move on until the Issue is Resolved
  - ○ Get to the root of the issue (5 Why? questions)
  - ○ Talk through possible solutions
- ➢ Resolve the issue one of two ways:
  - ○ Discuss in more depth without To-Dos associated; it is more like brainstorming.
  - ○ Make a To-Do for someone for 1 of 3 outcomes:
    - ▪ Gather more data and bring the data as an issue for the following week.
    - ▪ Create or update a process that was broken.
    - ▪ Work with someone on the team to ensure they understand the company's process and/or core values.
- ➢ Move to Issue 2 once you have a good path forward on Issue 1
- ➢ Repeat down the list

NOTE: Make sure that the *root* issue has been identified so that the To-Do will address the root issue and the issue will not come up again in the future. Don't rush this!

S.M.A.R.T Goals

The purpose of this template is not to enslave you to a rigid path. Instead, it is to capture the spirit of the objective and help us remember what we set out to do and why. That way, when your path does change, we can all remember and agree that we are still holding to the spirit and ambitious standards of the original idea.

Specific – What *exactly* are you trying to accomplish?

Measurable – What are the criteria for completion?

A quarter is thirteen weeks, so having a milestone every two is a good rule of thumb. Some goals may need more, some less. The schedule should reflect the plan above.

Achievable - What is your well-thought-out plan?

The best way to show that something is achievable is to lay out a plan to achieve it. "I'll start by making a plan" is code for "haven't thought this through."

Relevant – Why is this important?

Please describe the background story leading up to why this goal is relevant. If you don't write it down here, we run the risk of forgetting by the end of the quarter.

Timely – When is this going to be done?

Target Date: _____

Milestone Plan

Milestone	Target Date	Completed

Blockers, Resources, Obstacles and Reality

Imagine you failed. What was the reason?

What resources or people are you counting on?

Please give your plan to overcome any serious problems.

Delegation Matrix

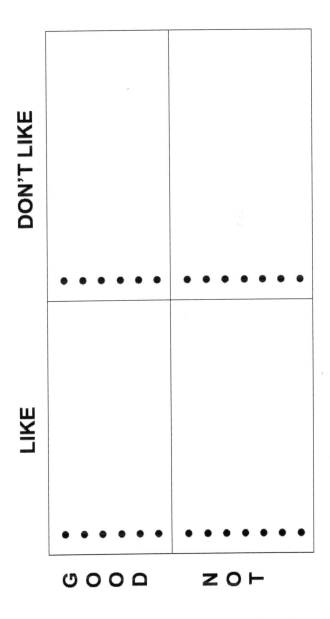

Roles & Responsibilities Chart

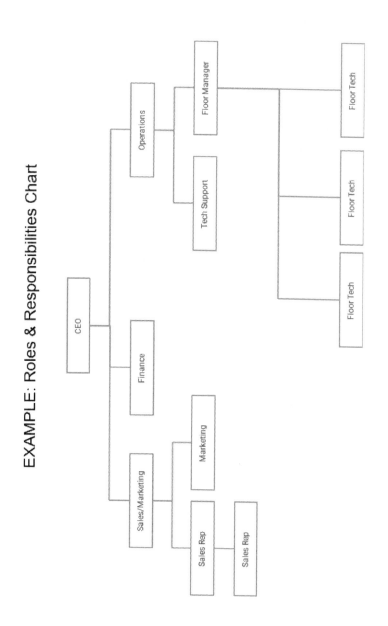

EXAMPLE: Roles & Responsibilities Chart

CEO

Sales/Marketing

Finance

Operations

Marketing

Sales Rep

Sales Rep

Tech Support

Floor Manager

Floor Tech

Floor Tech

Floor Tech

Core Values

To help define your culture through a small set of timeless and essential principles that guide the organization. These values are meant to attract people to your organization. They are the basis for reviewing, rewarding, hiring, firing, and recognizing employees.

Communication Guidelines

- **Rule of 7:** The Marketing Rule of 7 states that a prospect needs to "hear" the advertiser's message at least seven times before they take action to buy that product or service. It's a marketing maxim developed by the movie industry in the 1930s.

- **Simple Phrases, Deep Meaning:** Wordsmithing and developing the narrative of what the phrases mean so that it is clear to everyone who reads them.

- **Real World Examples:** Use stories and examples from your team that help solidify and bring the core values to life.

- **Exemplified by All:** These are called core values because they are the CORE of who the company is and what it represents. These core values are the basis for recognizing, rewarding, reviewing, hiring, and firing.

Core Values Examples

Unequivocal Excellence	Value of Reputation	Enthusiastic Tenacity
Courage to Do the Right Thing	Go the Extra Mile	Take Ownership
Hungry for Achievement	Put the Team First	Help People First
Individual Ability and Creativity	Innovative Problem Solver	Default Aggressive
No Entitlement	Think Like the Customer	Willing to Learn

Culture Check

Culture Check is a tool designed to help determine who fits the Core Values, Culture, and Competencies needed for the company and the role.

Ability – Are they competent in the position?

Desire – Do they want to be in that position?

Capacity – Can they handle the work required for the role?

CULTURE CHECK									ABILITY	DESIRE	CAPACITY
NAME											
THE BAR											

RATING: 👍 ✊ 👎

4 Strike Process (PIP Guidelines)

Occasionally, an employee may have a performance deficiency. We want to allow employees to correct their performance issues when possible and assist them. We also want to ensure we thoroughly investigate and handle serious offenses appropriately. The following is a guide, not a mandate. Use it when in doubt. Lack of effort on the employee's part or identification of a poor cultural fit should be handled in an accelerated process.

In those cases when we have an employee who is an excellent cultural fit but is failing to fulfill job requirements, our performance improvement plan has four steps:

Strike 0) When you first have a concern, this concern needs to be addressed as soon as possible and can be done informally. Set the expectations clearly with the employees so they know how and what to do to meet them.

Strike 1) Conference between the employee's manager and the employee, in which the manager addresses the concern with the employee and provides the employee with the expected corrective action. After this conversation, the manager writes up a description and provides a copy of this write-up to Human Resources for inclusion in the employee's personnel file.

Strike 2) Conference with the employee, the employee's manager, and a member of the Leadership Team and/or

Human Resources. In this conference, the employee will be presented with a written explanation of the problem and the expected corrective steps, which may include additional training.

The employee will be provided with a copy of this document and expected to sign a copy acknowledging receipt. The signed copy will be placed in the employee's personnel file. This begins the official 'Performance Improvement Plan' or PIP and notifies the employee that they are on probation.

The PIP is reviewed regularly with the employee to ensure the employee is on track to correct the issue. Once on a PIP, the employee does not get off the PIP for six months of sustained change. If the employee corrects the problem, after the 6-month timeline, the employee is presented with a written document crediting the employee with remedying the situation and removal from probation. If the employee is unable to perform to the standards and expectations outlined, then the employee moves to Strike 3

Strike 3) Third and final conference on the issue with the employee's manager and a member of the Leadership Team and/or Human Resources. In this conference, the employee will be presented with a written document explaining that the employee has not corrected the situation and terminating the employment relationship.

If the employment relationship is to be terminated, HR and the CEO should be notified before termination. The employee will receive a copy of this document, which will be placed in the employee's personnel file. An HR representative should be available during or after this meeting to help employees understand compensation issues. If you supervise employees, you are responsible for your employees' performance. You should mention a performance deficiency to the employee as part of your regular feedback if you know of a performance deficiency. If you determine that a performance improvement plan is the next step, work with your supervisor and/or human resources to ensure that the individual situation is handled appropriately.

The Author

Acknowledgments

"If you see a turtle on a fencepost, you know one thing for certain: he didn't get there by himself."

While I can't validate who said it first or where I first heard the saying, I resonate with it! There are so many people that I have learned from over the years: mentors, coaches, pastors, bosses, leaders, and friends. Here are a few who I am deeply thankful for and have helped me on my journey:

Anna – I love you. Thank you for being my best friend. I'm so blessed to have you in my life, cheering me on, believing in me, and never giving up on me, even in the darkest days.

Peyton and Torin – thanks for inspiring me to be a better man every day.

The Alyrica Team – where I understood what it takes to build a great company.

Kevin Sullivan – For believing in me when I wasn't sure about myself.

Joseph Sullivan – Thank you for sharing your mind with the world and for pushing me in ways that drive me to become more than I thought I could become.

And a **HUGE THANK YOU** to my editing team:

John Cassidy, Abigail Brown, Tony Sollars, JC Gayle, Andrew Phillips, and Tyler Redden.

About

Jason Richards is an entrepreneur, executive, and business strategist with a diverse background in various industries. Passionate about leadership, growth, and innovation, Jason has led and contributed to the success of several organizations throughout his career.

Driven by a passion for helping others succeed, Jason founded Leadcademy, a consulting company that empowers organizations and leaders to create effective strategies and processes for sustainable growth.

Most importantly, Jason is a husband, father, friend, and outdoor enthusiast.

This might be the first time you've heard about me, so if you're thinking... "Who is this Jason guy?"

Here are some highlights at the time of this writing:

- ➤ I'm 38 years old and have been in the business world for over 15 years.

- I started as a youth pastor when I was 19 years old… which didn't make much money, so I started some side businesses to help make ends meet.
- Like most upcoming entrepreneurs, I didn't know what I was doing when I started my first business (a painting company).
- I was fortunate to move from Seattle to Oregon and work with my cousins in several successful business ventures.
- A friend was visiting me from Montana (where I grew up) and saw how we structured and ran things and asked for help.
- I then created The Framework, which has helped companies across several industries simplify their company, get time back for the owner, and see significant growth in the process.

I don't like talking about myself, but I know some of you were wondering, so I had to get it out.

Now, I'd love to learn more about YOU.

Here is where you can find me online:

Fun and Professional on Instagram:

www.instagram.com/the_jasonrichards

Professional Life and Networking on LinkedIn:

www.linkedin.com/in/the-jason-richards

Websites About Leadcademy and Me:

www.leadcademy.com

www.thejasonrichards.com

A Shameless Plug

If you have got this far in the book, I'm guessing you have enjoyed it, even if just a little bit!

Could you do me a favor?

Amazon reviews are the gold standard for self-published books like this one.

Can you review this book on Amazon right now?

Since I'm asking, it would probably make sense to tell you how I may be able to help you in the future.

1) If you are a company that wants help implementing The Framework, we would be glad to see if a Framework Coach would be a good fit for your situation. Please email info@leadcademy.com.

2) Since I own the publishing rights, we can help you with bulk book orders and save you some serious $$.

3) We can also customize the cover and branding as a service to speaking clients and would love to discuss the opportunity to do the same for you. Please email speaking@thejasonrichards.com, where we can set up a time to chat.

Shameless plug concluded: thanks for taking the time to be with me. I hope to connect with you soon!

Made in the USA
Columbia, SC
16 April 2025

56742065R00102